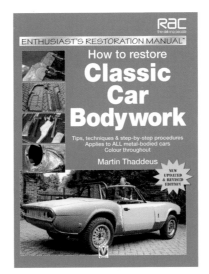

rac
the driving people

ENTHUSIAST'S RESTORATION MANUAL

How to restore

Classic Car Bodywork

Tips, techniques & step-by-step procedures
Applies to ALL metal-bodied cars
Colour throughout

Martin Thaddeus

NEW
UPDATED
& REVISED
EDITION

OTHER GREAT BOOKS FROM VELOCE –

www.veloce.co.uk

First published in 2004, reprinted April 2006 & December 2008, new updted and revised edition April 2012 by Veloce Publishing Limited, Veloce House, Parkway Farm Business Park, Middle Farm Way, Poundbury, Dorchester, Dorset, DT1 3AR, England. Fax 01305 250479/e-mail info@veloce.co.uk/web www.veloce.co.uk or www.velocebooks.com.

ISBN: 978-1-845844-11-0 UPC: 6-36847-04411-4

ENTHUSIAST'S RESTORATION MANUAL™

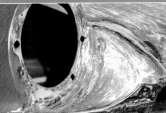

How to restore
Classic
Car
Bodywork

Tips, techniques & step-by-step procedures
Applies to ALL metal-bodied cars
Colour throughout

Martin Thaddeus

NEW UPDATED & REVISED EDITION

VELOCE

Contents

Introduction

This book was written for all those classic car enthusiasts who want to get involved with bodywork, but who, for whatever reason, feel they lack the necessary knowledge or confidence. Although I've met many owners and enthusiasts over the years who would readily get involved with the mechanics of their beloved vehicle, most would shy away from any panel work as if it were something of a 'black art.'

While it's true that some panel beaters have a touch of the prima-donna about them, magic, of course, doesn't come into it. What I really want to get across in this book is the fact that, whatever I can do, you can do, too ... albeit with a little help.

When you've reskinned a hundred doors, you're not going to be fazed by number 101. On the other hand, if the results of your first attempts are to hang on the car of your dreams, you might find this a slightly bigger deal. Not to worry, though, I still remember my first attempts, and I have subsequently talked enough people through the process to be familiar with the snags you're likely to encounter (and how to get around them).

These days, it increasingly seems to be the case that panel repair means panel replacement. Many of the older skills are being lost, and craftsmanship has given way to mass-production. To my mind, however, the body man who doesn't understand the nature and properties of the metal he is working is always going to be at a disadvantage.

With regard to the range of vehicles this book will cover, I'm aiming for the middle ground. That's to say; not the

Intro-1a. Before, as found in a scrapyard. ...

Intro-1b. ... and after, showing anything is possible.

earliest carriages with wood or canvas coachwork, and not the costliest, hand-made, light alloy one-offs. The cars with which I'm most familiar, and the cars most commonly owned, are the mass-produced, steel-bodied vehicles built in the fifties, sixties and seventies. The nature of metal, though, is such that anyone, with any vehicle of any age, will probably find something of use in the following pages.

Enthusiasm is a key element in any restoration project, but you should bear in mind that it's very easy to be enthusiastic when things are going well. There may be days when things go badly, of course, and other days when no progress is made at all. Bodywork, too, is not without its hazards, and safety must always be at the forefront of your mind. A book can only take you so far, and I will point out the potential dangers as they arise, but there's no substitute for common sense, and you would do well to speak to as many people who have been involved in this kind of work as you can.

In writing this book, I have assumed that the reader will have no specialist knowledge and no specialist equipment or plant. Over the years I have worked in main dealerships and in my own little shop, and pretty much everything in between. I have also, on occasion, worked out of the back of my jeep, at the homes of my customers. Such situations limited the techniques that I could employ, and forced me to develop ways of working without the aid of many of the tools which are central to the big shop. The techniques that I developed are, therefore, perfect for the home restorer who doesn't have access to full bodyshop facilities. This, coupled with my love of bringing the owners into the restoration process in a very hands-on way, places me in a good position to write a work which aims to bridge some of the divide between amateur and professional.

SCOPE OF THE BOOK
The projects covered in this book reflect the sort of problems you are likely to encounter during the course of a normal restoration. To some extent, the jobs you can handle are governed by the tools you have to hand and your own ingenuity. By way of an example, I once made a side panel section for a Toyota Space Cruiser (Lite-Ace). This section spanned the area between the wheelarches, and from the waistline down to the sill. The problem, however, was that all I had to hand was a small folding work bench, a length of 2x4, and a friend. I'm not suggesting that you have your mates stand on your sheet metal while you work it, of course, merely that sometimes we have to improvise.

This is not a book on panel development, though I can offer a

Intro-2. GT6 awaits restoration after more than 30 years of patching.

good foundation in that discipline. I will show you how to make wing and floor sections, rather than complete wings and floorpans.

Likewise, this is not a book on welding, though I will outline many welding techniques. You should bear in mind that MIG and oxyacetylene equipment represent a huge potential danger to both person and property. In some parts of Europe, for example, welding gas is classed as an explosive! It would be foolish, therefore, to attempt to learn to weld from books alone. Instead, it would be far better, and safer, to cover the basics with an experienced welder.

BUYING YOUR CLASSIC VEHICLE
There are many issues that must be addressed before you embark on a major restoration project. Your choice of vehicle, for example, and the way you approach the job at every stage will depend on many factors. These include the importance you place on originality, whether the cost and effort is reflected in the ultimate value of the car (after all, the workload involved in restoring a Morris Minor may be the same as that for a Ferrari), whether you regard the restoration as a financial investment, and, of course, what you can afford. There's also the availability of parts to consider.

The reasons for choosing to purchase any particular vehicle are as numerous as there are models to choose from. Firstly, what is a classic? I gave up trying to answer that one years ago. Some cars gain classic status because nobody could ever afford them, while others are now desirable because everybody and his uncle had one. My old Ford Anglia, for example, was, and is, worth nothing. I had always regarded the model as ugly, but driving the thing made every journey an adventure. Not least because, wherever I went, people would point and wave, and, more often than not, I'd have someone walk over saying, "Cor blimey, I had one of them," and, "Fantastic, yeah, oh that's made my day." In truth, I would never have actually chosen the 'Anglebox,' in fact, but took it simply because it was convenient at the time. Today, though, I would happily recommend an Anglia to anybody. It's practical to own and cheap to run, though, of course, it will never make any money. Wings for this model, however, are very rare, and can cost far more than a complete car to buy.

Generally, the more popular a model is today, the better the parts situation, regardless of the value. Supply has followed demand. The 'bubble market' of the mid-eighties and early-nineties has done much to increase awareness that the classic car is an investment. At the same time, however, it has left many wary

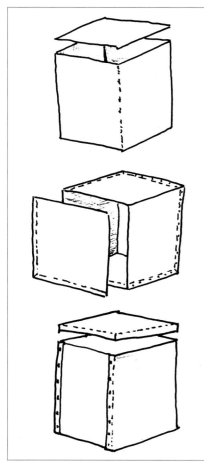

How would you build a box?

of getting their fingers burnt. It seems that, in Britain at least, people are looking to the domestic classic rather than the exotic. These days, the classic car world is once again led by enthusiasts rather than speculators, and to my mind, that can only be a good thing.

My advice for choosing a make and model is, go with your heart, but let your brain have its say! Buy the car you want to live with, but do your homework first, and choose the best of its type you can afford. Alternatively, buy a rough one, but in the full knowledge of what it needs to bring it up to scratch.

VEHICLE CONSTRUCTION

For the novice restorer getting the job right is often a matter of not getting it wrong. Before you start pulling bits off your car, it's a good idea to understand what holds it together, and how it was made. For example, imagine you have six sheets of steel 3ft (1m) square, and 20swg (0.7mm thick). Bring the sheets together in your mind to form a cube, and consider how you would join the seams. The obvious answer might be to weld along the edges where they meet. Although this would do for a one-off, it would be far too slow and costly for the likes of Henry Ford. It would also be difficult to control the heat distortion. You might consider adding an extra $\frac{1}{2}$in or so around each edge, and turned out at 45 degrees. This new edge would make it easier to handle and locate the panels, and, with a spot welder, we could join them without any appreciable distortion (and in a tiny fraction of the time it would take to seam weld).

This method works well to a point, but if we scale the box up, we'd probably find that the sides are a bit floppy and the seams are starting to warp. We could use a thicker material to counter this, but that would make it heavier and costlier, of course. We could form a little shape into the panels. A very slight crown, for example, would add enough tension to hold the side panels in shape without altering the edges. Alternatively, we could roll a curve into some or all of our sides, though this would require some tinkering with the seams, but it would add to the strength.

Those external seams might be

The horseless carriage.

regarded as a bit ugly, though, so we might want to turn the seams inward. We can't close the box from the outside in the same way, of course, but the result is much neater, and we could lose some seam edges if we wanted and weld directly onto some panels, thus saving more weight. Also, if we welded top-hat sections under the floor and around the periphery ... I think you get the picture. Now you can see why vehicle manufacturers invest so much time building concealed seams into their products.

The stresses which your vehicle is built to withstand far exceed simply its own weight and yours. Your car must be able to carry its engine, suspension, doors, trim, payload, and you, safely. And the doors have to open when you get there! Your classic car is probably made up from about one to two hundred individual pressings, many of which are hidden, and all of which (hopefully), work together to form a homogenous structure.

It's useful to look at the earliest carriages to understand how the modern vehicle has developed. Imagine an old style coach, for example, with its iron chassis, cart springs, wooden wheels with iron rims, and that wood frame and canvas body. This is pretty close to the very first cars (or horseless carriages). The first pressed steel chassis and glass windscreens appeared in 1903, with pneumatic tyres about the same time, though a look at any typical motor car of this time makes it clear that the construction of body and chassis still employed coach-building techniques for some time.

The Ford Model T was first sold in 1908, and its nineteen year production run spanned a time of great change in design and styling. Though the old Tin Lizzie was primarily a utilitarian beast, many modifications had to be incorporated in order for it to keep up with the competition. It was usual for vehicles of this era to be sold with a choice of plywood, canvas, or sheet-metal (or any combination), stretched over a wooden frame which sat on a ladder type steel

Intro-3. A fairly famous rally car restored – Tony Pond's ex-works TR7 V8.

chassis. Body style and type varied hugely, and might be saloon, coupé, or lightweight for racing. The build methods still employed by the Morgan company follow these lines today, a Belgian ash frame with alloy panels pinned onto it sits atop a steel ladder chassis. Not state of the art, but still a lot of fun.

While Morgan may exist in something of a time warp, the rest of the world has moved on. Wood has given way to steel for the underpinnings, with more steel for the skin, and mass-production techniques devised during the second world war moved development on a pace. Resistance spot welding sped up build rates and lowered costs, and in Europe and Japan, the separate chassis began to disappear, giving way to integral construction.

The separate chassis has remained, though, and it's only in the first years of the twenty-first century that we see it finally bow out, due mainly to safety concerns in the American market. A close inspection of many early integral chassis models will reveal the designs to be little more than a separate chassis body with a top-hat box section running the length of the floor, with perhaps the odd outrigger communicating to the sills.

A few years ago, I was working on a 1967 Bentley and a 1967 Cadillac. These two automobiles represented the ultimate in luxury from both sides of the Atlantic. They also stood diametrically opposed in terms of design and construction concepts. The Bentley sat upon a huge chassis that would have been at home on a steam engine, the floor bulkhead and suspension mounts where of steel, the A- and B-posts (and much of the superstructure), were of timber, and the outer skin was hand-crafted aluminium. The Bentley had the air of a gentleman's club on wheels, and it reeked of craftsmanship and days gone by.

The Cadillac, in contrast, was of all-steel construction. It also sat upon a substantial separate chassis, though this was a more modern, peripheral affair, which allowed the body to sit lower down. The quality of the panels was something of a revelation to me. As an Englishman, I had expected the 'Yank-tank' to be all flash and no substance. How wrong could I be, the metal was of unbelievable resilience and finish, while the amount of industrial capacity employed to manufacture one wing could have produced half a VW Beetle!

The point is that some production methods have continued, even though they have been superseded. The 1967 Bentley would be recognisable to a turn-of-the-century coachbuilder, while the Cadillac would not tax today's panel

beater. The age of your car will not always reflect the era of its making.

MILD STEEL SHEET
As small-time consumers our choice of material is confined to the range carried by our local motor factors or welding supply outlet, which, in my experience, is limited at best. Mild steel traditionally comes in full sheets of 8ft x 4ft and half sheets of 4ft x 4ft. Pre-formed L sections and box sections are also supplied by some outlets.

Sheet thickness should reflect popular applications, so expect to be offered 18 and 20swg, though a check with a wire gauge will often reveal the true

sizes to be anything from 17 to 22swg claiming to be 20swg. Your sheet will often come coated with some sort of protective layer, whether requested or not. Try to avoid galvanised sheet, though, as it spits when welded.

Surface tension
To make handling easier, your sheet will have been hot and cold rolled. This process imparts surface tension, which can be removed by re-rolling or annealing (heating). Surface tension is an important factor in modern vehicle construction, all of those curves and crowns are not there just to please the eye, and actively holds

Intro-4a. A pile of new metal ...

Intro-4b. ... becomes a car. This Spit is ready for the paintshop.

Intro-5a. This award-winning 3.9ltr V8 supercar ...

Intro-5b. ... was once less splendid. It now comprises a lot of new metal.

the vehicle in shape. Likewise, the deep draw pressings that make up the pillars and posts have gentle twists and tapers which do more then just look good. As a rule, there are no straight lines on your car, though some may be pretty close (often, what appears straight in one plane probably curves in another).

When sheet steel is hammered, bent, or shaped, it tends to work-harden and, if overworked, will become brittle. However, annealing can be used to normalise the metal to allow further working. Modern steels can be produced to allow deeper and easier pressing, these new alloys also allow much thinner gauges to be used without loss of strength.

SPOT WELDS & SPOT WELDING

Resistance spot welding was accidentally invented in 1877, though it was not widely used industrially until the 1930s. The process, in its simplest form, involves fusing a small spot or nugget of metal across two sheets of steel by use of pressure and a current passed through two copper electrodes. In production, multiple electrode welders machines can weld entire seams in one hit, and other roller-type electrode machines can produce continuous seams, such as roof/gutter seams.

A simple hand-operated resistance spot welder can be acquired at reasonable cost, and is the easiest and safest method of producing welds. This is also the method used in the original manufacture and there is little or no risk of distortion involved.

Intro-6a to Intro-6c. Spot welded seams.

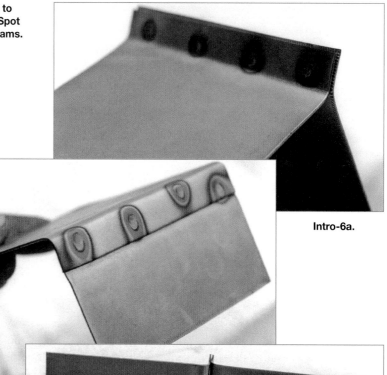

Intro-6a.

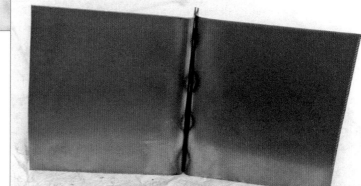

Intro-6b.

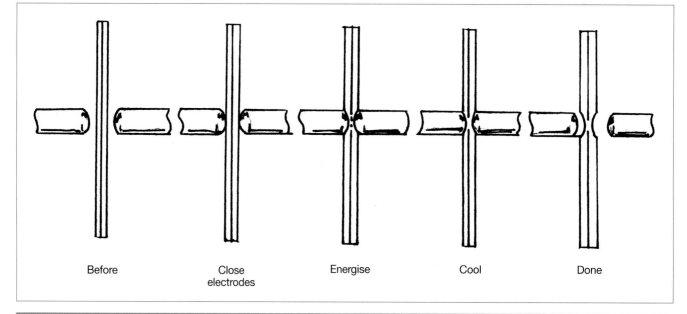

Intro-6c.

Forming a resistance spot weld.

| Before | Close electrodes | Energise | Cool | Done |

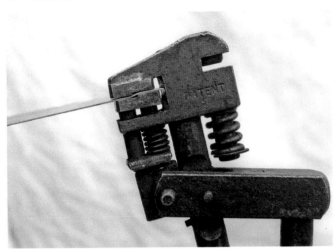

Intro-9a. Flush seam. Joddler and spot welder have been used to create a clean join mid-panel.

Intro-7. Joddler allows easy formation of flush seams.

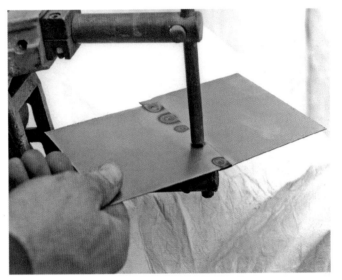

Intro-8. Joddled and punched. A joddler/punch is invaluable.

Intro-9b. Spot welder.

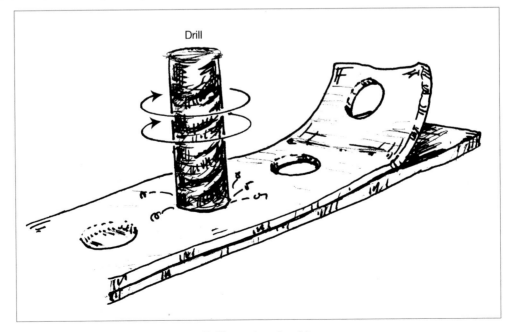

Drill

Drilling out spot welds.

Chapter 1

Rust – know your enemy

Because iron doesn't naturally exist in the metallic form with which we are familiar, and since steel is basically iron, rusting should be regarded simply as iron returning to its more natural, oxidised state. While this might be a nuisance, we should remember that the same affinity between iron and oxygen is what allows us to breath – so don't knock it!

In practical terms, rusting occurs when steel is exposed to air and water. In England, for example, where the air is damp and the rain is acidic, steel will always rust if not actively protected. Welding will always attract corrosion partly because most seams involve an overlap or some other form of water trap. Welding is also prone to rusting due to what is called intergranular corrosion. This means that the metal surrounding any weld is disrupted by the heating process on a microscopic, granular level. In the case of a spot weld, for example, the metal around the weld will reach about 800 degrees Celsius, while the weld centre will get much hotter and the material further out will stay cool. This also explains how it is that we can 'wiggle' a weld apart while leaving the centre intact. The heat disruption has removed the surface tension.

Another factor to consider is stress-induced corrosion. Steel will work – harden if repeatedly vibrated; the hardened area is similar to the intergranular state, and will attract corrosion. The areas most prone to this form of attack are also likely to be weld seams and, therefore, water traps.

It's not always possible to prevent water from entering a car's body. The doors, for example, will generally not be sealed around a drop glass. In such cases, therefore, it's important that the water be allowed to pass out of the structure at the same rate at which it enters. Water which is allowed to sit will seep into the finest crevice, and run by capillary action wherever it can.

1-1. Water and gravity – water traps lead to rusting!

Road spray and condensation are other factors for consideration.

Much of your car's destruction will slowly take place behind what appears to be sound metal, so by the time it bubbles through it might be quite extensive. This is particularly true in the case of chassis outriggers, which can lose a lot of material

1-2. How many sills? Original, plus two!

and strength, while still looking well on the outside.

When assessing a car's structure, the only foolproof method is destructive testing. Not surprisingly, not all prospective vendors will go along with this idea.

PROTECTION
The primary protection of any car, of course, is its paintwork. Any surface not painted must, therefore, be otherwise coated, and any new paint should be firmly based on a rust inhibitor, such as an etch primer.

It's imperative that we consider rust protection at every stage of the restoration process if our efforts are not to be wasted in the long-term. Many rust treatments are phosphoric acid-based or zinc-based, which makes them toxic. You should always treat these substances with due respect and in accordance with

1-3. Repair upon repair. Old metal encourages more rot.

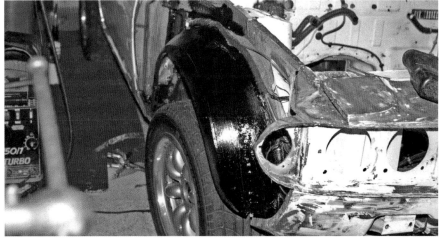

1-5. Underseal inside the wing area before wing is fitted.

1-4. Zinc spray between seams and over weld.

1-6. Primer and sealer keep the moisture off the metal prior to painting.

the warnings provided. Etch primers will promote adhesion and treat your metal surface. Zinc sprays are useful for welded areas, and in between seams, though some etch primers will not stick to zinc chromate so you would be well advised to consult your sprayer or paint supplier before purchase. Zinc-based red oxide primers are ideal for protecting your project while it is in the shop. Your painter can always take it off if he chooses.

Brushable mastic sealers and their cartridge gun counterparts are invaluable when it comes to keeping water out. Use only good quality, branded products, and remember that polyurethane bonding sealer will draw moisture out of a seam as it cures. It will also stick anything it contacts.

Wax injection is the most popular rust inhibitor, though it is only suitable for use after the structural work and paintwork have been completed as the wax is highly inflammable and will interfere with paint

adhesion. Wax injection is also a very smelly and messy business, best carried out in a well ventilated area away from the neighbours and any soft trim.

Rubberised mastic sprays, known as stone chip, are widely used on modern cars. Available in smooth and textured forms, they can be aerosol or gun applied, and then painted over. Though not strictly 'original,' many classic car owners opt for the extra protection these products offer.

The best modern underseals are wax-based and can be brush or gun applied, though either way you're going to get dirty. Products such as wax injection take some time to dry and will smell for a few days, during which time they remain flammable and prone to dripping.

Finally, remember that a draughty but dry barn can often protect a car better than a sealed heated garage. Air, even damp air, has an affinity for water, and will tend to dry out a car's structure. Likewise, 1970s underseal will often have dried out

and split. This, then, encourages water to creep along the floor, causing more problems than it might have prevented. Modern underseals, on the other hand, remain waxy and flexible, and many have a 'creepant' action which will cover any breach in the protective film.

1-7. Red oxide protects well and can be removed by the painter if desired.

Chapter 2
Tools, equipment & workspace

The scope of what you can hope to achieve is, to a great extent, governed by where you work and what equipment you use. Although ingenuity also plays its part here, in my opinion, creativity tends to be born out of experience.

BASIC TOOLS
Hand tools
Panel work will always involve some fitting and stripping or general mechanical work, so you'll need all the normal tools for servicing, etc. Bear in mind that top price doesn't necessarily mean top value, though better quality items are often thinner and, therefore, more versatile. Budget tools, though, have improved hugely in recent years. Also, bear in mind that top price doesn't mean that the tools are unbreakable or can't be lost!

• Sockets and spanners. Metric and/or AF depending on your model. $1/4$ and $3/8$ inch drive sockets, in standard and deep form, are a must, as are an assortment of extensions. Good quality ratchets and budget sockets will get you by without breaking the bank.

• Pliers and grips. Grab any and all. Again, a few good items will pay dividends as they will allow good purchase in situations of limited access. A good pair of swan-neck pliers will become indispensable.

• Monkey-wrenches are very handy, so collect a range of sizes.

• Mole-type self-grip wrenches are a must, you cannot have too many. Include flat and three-fingered welding clamps and assorted C-clamps.

• Screwdrivers. A good budget set will generally surfice, but buy a decent magnetic ratchet. You'll also need a couple of heavy gauge drivers and couple of long reach items – everything in flat blade and cross-head. As things progress, you may also find the need for watch makers' sets and impact drivers.

• Crowbars and drifts. Pry bars and levers are indispensable. Over the years I have collected (and lost), all manner of metal bits and bobs for applying leverage and force (many were custom made). Old steering columns are an excellent starting point. Also, buy a trim-fork.

• Panel beating gear. Hammers and dollies are the mainstay of panel beating. In theory you can never have too many combinations, though in practice you'll wind up using only a couple or so. Budget starter sets are often good value, but don't expect too much from the lower price range. Don't let yourself be easily charmed by flashy top-branded gear, though; after all, we're only talking about weighted sticks. I have to admit to owning

a Snap-On shrinking hammer that cost me a lot of money back in the 1980s – and it is brilliant. Pictures 2-1 to 2-6 show what you can regard as the minimum set.

• Hammers. A light bumping hammer with round and square faces; a heavy bumping hammer with a round face and cross pien; and another heavy with a round face and pick.

• Dollies. Flat (toe), round, heel, and either a comma or double-ended dolly.

• T-stakes. T-stakes are polished and rounded sections of metal rod in various sizes, which are mounted on stakes. They are designed for use in the vice, but are jolly handy when hand-held. Unfortunately, T-stakes are pretty pricey, so it's best to make them if you need them.

• Round billet. A section of 4 inch rod, cut to a 2 inch length is excellent for cold shrinking. Scrounge a piece from your local steel works.

• Miscellaneous beating gear. You'll also need a heavy hammer for roughing out and drift work. A heavy engineer's ball pien, a club hammer and a rawhide mallet are all useful for this.

• Special hammers. Many 'wonder hammers' are on offer, dont buy them! Instead, get a bumping file – which was

2-1. A range of hammers.

2-4. Bumping file and body file.

2-2. Dollies and blocks.

2-5. Hammer box.

2-3. T-stake, spoon, pry bar, etc.

2-6. A few clamps.

traditionally an old file bent for slapping – the gnarled face grips the metal.

• Spoons. Invest in a universal spoon. This is used for dolly work in restricted areas, and is also a good lever. Again, making spoons is an option.

• Spring hammer. Basically, this is half a cart spring shaped for slapping and for use in combination with a heavy hammer. The spring hammer is laid flat on the raised area and the hammer is brought down onto it. This method dissipates the blow resulting in movement without further damage. The effect is greatly magnified if the damaged area of metal is held in tension.

• Slide hammer. The slide hammer is a metal shaft with a handle on one end and either a coarse screw or a hook on the other (a weight runs between them). The device is used by fixing one end to a dent and applying tension to the handle, then sharply sliding the weight backwards. The result is a reverse impact. Many variations of the slide hammer exist, including the 'Rospot,' a device which welds a nail onto the panel, and which has a special slide hammer for pulling them out.

• Metal cutting gear. You can never have too many tools for cutting metal, and the more options you have the better.

• Snips. Aviation-type snips are a must. Purchase right, left, and straight cut types, but stick to middle price or budget items.

Gilbow-type snips are also handy, and a roller type cutter is worth its weight in gold. The 'Sykes mini cutter' that I use is brilliant.

• Pen, cut, and nibbler attachments for your drill are worthwhile, if not essential.

• Vice and bench. A really solid bench is a must, though at a pinch you can get

2-7. For bumping alloy panels.

2-10. Vice bench and block.

2-8. Hole punch/joddler.

2-11. Electric spot welder.

2-9. Sykes mini-cutter.

2-12. MIG welder.

away with using a workmate-type folding bench with a board fixed into the jaws. A decent bench vice is also very desirable, the best ones have an anvil type area. As well as a bench and a vice, you'll also want a beating block which, in its simplest form, is a piece of steel plate, about 300mm x 300mm x 6mm, and a section of RSJ for use as an anvil. You'll find miscellaneous metal blocks of great worth as things progress.

A visit to your local steel fabricator is very worthwhile, especially as he may agree to supply you with steel at cost. A root around in the dumpster, though, should provide you with your anvil, beating block, spring hammer, and enough odds and sods to make any drift or tool you require. Short bits of pipe or bar will give billets for shaping, or allow you to make T-stakes. Ask permission first, though, and expect to pay a couple of quid for the privilege. Watch out for sharp edges!

• Jacks, etc. You'll want at least one decent trolley jack. The odd scissor jack will prove handy and one or two pairs of sturdy axle stands are a must. I also use wooden safety blocks. If you're going to get into sill replacement or serious structural work, then you'll need at least one expanding door aperture brace. These are generally sold in pairs.

Hydraulic gear
Porto-power hydraulic ram sets are useful, but not usually essential. If you do buy one, shop around, as prices vary hugely.

Power tools
I will assume that you're not in a position to employ air tools so, for now, we'll look at the electric options.

• Angle grinder. Buy a decent 4$\frac{1}{2}$ inch angle grinder at about a 550/650 watt rating. Any smaller and it will struggle, any hotter and it will kick like a mule. You'll also want cutting, grinding and fibre discs. Your grinder will take a lot of punishment, so chose a reliable one with a locking button as this saves hunting for the keys all the time.

• Drill. Modern cordless drills save having another cable trailing across the workshop, but only the heavier models can cope with all you'll want of a drill. I opt for a light cordless one for screw driving and odd jobs, with a decent power drill for the big stuff.

Buy a budget drill set, along with a cone-drill and a bunch of 3.5mm bits for use with pop rivets and PKs.

Welding gear
For most home restorers, MIG welders will cover most jobs. Gas welding is largely regarded as being somewhat archaic these days, while electric spot welders are considered industrial.

• Gas. Oxyacetylene welding gear in the right hands can be a joy to behold. In the wrong hands, however, this equipment can be extremely dangerous. If you intend to employ gas welding, then it's imperative that you take good instruction from an expert. It's also essential that you read up on the local by-laws governing the control of such equipment. This said, small Porto-pack welding sets are available for the low use consumer. Oxyacetylene is more commonly used for burning off paint and underseal rather than welding these days, though a decent, single-handed blow torch or heat gun is far safer.

• MIG. MIG welding is a form of shielded arc welding and has become the new mainstay of restoration.Though less 'authentic' than gas, the convenience and relative safety of MIG make it a good choice. When buying a MIG welder, choose a machine rated at about 120-180 amps. What makes a good welder is not big power, but stable power. Ask about the 'duty-cycle,' the greater the percentage of time at or near your desired amperage, the more stable your arc will be. Invest in a self-darkening visor, as this will give the best protection, while improving your welding ability no end.

• Electric spot welder. The resistance spot welder is the most original and convenient way to form welds on any car. The use of the conventional spot weld machine is limited, though, as it requires good access to both sides of the join. The latest generation of single-sided welders are ideal for restoration, but are very pricey! Light industrial machines can be picked up fairly cheaply from reputable bodyshops that have upgraded their equipment.

The ideal set-up would be to have access to all three forms of welding. If you opt for only one then it has to be MIG. If you can also afford the electric welder, it will save a lot of time and hassle.

• The Rospot is a very clever device for electrically welding pins onto panels (the pins are then pulled with a slide hammer). When fitted with a different electrode, which is supplied, the Rospot can be used for shrinking excess metal.

While this piece of equipment is intended for professional bodyshop use, as a restorer I find it no end of use.

THE WORKSPACE
Vehicle restoration can be a hugely rewarding pastime, it can also be dirty, smelly, dangerous, claustrophobic and very frustrating. Don't handicap yourself further by attempting to work in cold, dark, wet, or cramped conditions.

• Space. Ideally, your workspace should be big enough for your car, of course, allow plenty of room to move around it, and also accommodate your workbench. This space should be well ventilated, warm, dry and well lit. Do not underestimate the value of good lighting.

• Location. Your workspace should be in a position where your chosen pastime does not intrude into other people's lives. Machine noise and chemical fumes cause more offence then you might think.

• Utilities. Electricity is key. A feeble extension lead will not feed your welder and lighting simultaneously. Water is nice too, of course, but you can bring your own at a push.

• Safety considerations. Will it catch fire? What if I catch fire? Can I get help? Does it leak? Will I poison the neighbours; and will they sue?

2-13. To work – don't handicap yourself with a poor workspace.

Chapter 3
Workshop safety

Every aspect of panel work poses at least some degree of risk to life or limb. You MUST be aware of each risk factor as it presents itself, and take care not to let your vigilance lapse. Safety considerations do, of course, extend beyond your own health, so bear in mind that **your** personal standards of acceptable risk may not be shared by your neighbours or the wider community.

In Britain, for example, many of the materials and processes employed in bodywork are governed by the Control of Substances Hazardous to Health Act (COSHH). These regulations demand that all workshops make yearly detailed assessments of every potentially hazardous substance in stock. Paints, solvents, cleaning materials and fillers are all considered as hazardous, as are dusts and grinds produced by abrasion. Appropriate protection must, according to COSHH, be employed at all times, as must suitable extraction, filtration and flameproof lighting.

Although an element of judgement must be employed when using bodywork tools, techniques and materials, you must take great care not to contravene the safety regulations.

SPECIFIC HAZARDS
Welding
• MIG. MIG welders are heavy, cumbersome machines with electrical cables attached. The most unwieldy thing about them, though, is the gas bottle, which tends to make the machines top heavy. This metal cylinder stores Argon/ CO_2 at about 3000psi. Both these gases are oxygen depleters and, therefore, potential asphyxiants. The gases are fed out of the bottle via a relatively weak brass regulator which, if broken, would allow a massive high pressure discharge of the contents.

A new set of dangers appear when the machine is in operation, of course. The tip of the welding torch is 'live' when the trigger is pressed, as is the wire which feeds from it. When the wire strikes an earthed object (the workpiece), an electrical arc and an amount of white hot molten metal are produced.

• Resistance spot welding. The spot welder is another heavy and awkward machine with a trailing electrical flex. Usage often demands that it be held for long periods in difficult and uncomfortable positions. Take up a well balanced stance and don't allow the hot electrodes to touch anything they shouldn't.

Triggering the welder closes the electrodes and passes a high voltage across the arms. This should be conducted away through the machine, of course, but will earth via the easiest route. If the path of least resistance is your gold wedding band and the puddle you're standing in, then that's the route it will take; so keep your wits about you!

• Oxyacetylene. Oxygen is stored in bottles at about 4500psi at room temperature. The gas is fed to the torch via a brass regulator and a rubber hose. Any grease or organic matter which is exposed to pure oxygen at this pressure will oxidise and vaporise with dramatic results, so don't allow anything into the bottle neck –

Safety is a state of mind.

even a dirty finger! Any leak of oxygen will increase the risk of fire enormously and, if it's heated, the pressure in the gas bottle will rise dangerously. Some years ago, a British Oxygen Company truck caught fire locally and, when the bottles exploded, some took off and were found a mile away!

Acetylene is a highly explosive gas. It is stored in solution with acetone which, in turn, is held in a gauze packing inside a gas bottle. Acetylene is unstable above 2bar (30psi) so it's imperative that it remain in solution and in its gauze. This is why it's important to keep acetylene bottles upright at all times. Your supplier will provide you with handling information.

When in use, oxyacetylene produces a flame which is not readily visible through welding goggles for its whole length. This form of welding also tends to impart more unwanted heat into the workpiece and, by comparison with both MIG and spot, it comes with an increased risk of both fire and personal injury.

A spark gun should always be employed for igniting oxyacetylene. You should never keep matchboxes or cigarette lighters in the workshop, as sparks may breach their outer casings resulting in a flare-up or blast. A single disposable lighter in close proximity to the body can kill on detonation. Consideration must also be given to the use, storage and disposal of solvents. A carelessly discarded thinners rag, for example, has caught out many a panel man over the years.

POWER TOOLS

The two most frequently used power tools are the angle grinder and the drill. Both are clumsy items, which often require both hands to operate accurately. It's essential, therefore, that a proper balance and stance be adopted when using these machines to avoid damage to yourself or your work. Both machines generate a torque reaction, and both produce hazardous waste in the form of fumes and metal particles. The grinder, of course, will always create hot sparks which, if their direction is not controlled, can ignite trim or trousers.

You should also watch out for sharp burrs along metal edges. **Never** run your finger along the edge of any panel, seam or drilling.

Parts separated from a vehicle by cutting or drilling must be controlled and supported to avoid damage to self and property. Such parts can be very heavy, and always have sharp edges.

Mains-powered machinery obviously requires the use of cables which, apart from the electrical risk, also pose a tripping hazard.

Abrasive discs if improperly used (using the wrong disk for the job, for example, or snagging a fibre disk on a panel edge), may burst with dramatic results. Dust and grinds may also be toxic or offensive. Consider your ventilation or extraction carefully, and always wear a mask.

HAND TOOLS

Beating a metal structure with weighted sticks and lumps of iron is rife with potential hazards. Dropped, deflected or inaccurately aimed tools may seem funny in sitcoms, for example, but a lump hammer bouncing of a boot lid onto the

Focus on the job in hand.

forehead is not so funny when that head is your own. I've witnessed this and it's no joke. Anything with the potential to reshape steel obviously has a huge potential for inflicting personal injury.

Always think before you strike, and check your balance and counter-hold – this term usually refers to your dolly hand, but, to some extent, the term also refers to whichever foot is in front of your body – as you may find yourself pushing back on it to move out of the way of an errant tool or panel.

Safety is a state of mind: be constantly vigilant and always try to think ahead in terms of whether the way you intend to tackle a job is likely to put you in danger or, perhaps, result in damage to the vehicle.

Chapter 4
Basic panel removal

The principles of panel removal and replacement hold true for any panel. Removing a structural member or the roof, however, will obviously require special considerations beyond that of removing a simple wing. Nevertheless, your wing, sill and roof are attached using the same methods, and will require the same techniques to replace.

A VERY SIMPLE PANEL

This deck panel sits between the tonneau cover and the boot lid. It is attached by spot welds which, for the most part, are easily accessible when the adjacent panels are unbolted. The welds at either side, however, are concealed, and the seam that they form is a bit of a water trap. A small amount of braze has been used to supplement the spot welds where the panel joins to the boot aperture.

This small panel is easily replaced, though care is needed since any misalignment will result in fouling of the boot lid and/or the tonneau cover. The quality of the replacement panel is not brilliant in this case, so I've put location marks on the adjacent panels at each end.

The exposed spot welds are now drilled out, leaving the base metal intact. The seams at the side cannot be drilled until after the bulk of the panel has been removed, so an incision is made using a cutting disc on a grinder just inside the seam, and this is continued, using a hacksaw, into the boot aperture on the

inside of the overlap. In theory, the old panel will now fall off. In reality, however, it will probably need a little bit more persuasion. If necessary, split around the lower crease of the panel with a sharp mortise chisel.

Once the panel is free and can be removed (with care), any remnants of the seam weld can be lifted with a chisel and mole grips. Very stubborn bits, or any traces of braze, can be ground off, taking care not remove any of the base metal.

FRONT WING

A car's front wings are its most vulnerable panels and, as such, the most frequently replaced. As a jobbing tin-basher of many years standing, I have straightened more offside fronts than I wish to remember.

Pictures 4-1a to 4-1k. Wing replacement sequence.

4-1b. True state of wing.

4-1a. Stripping trim.

4-1c. Drill out weld on door edge ...

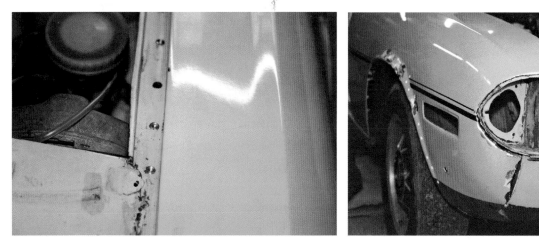
4-1d. ... and in engine bay.

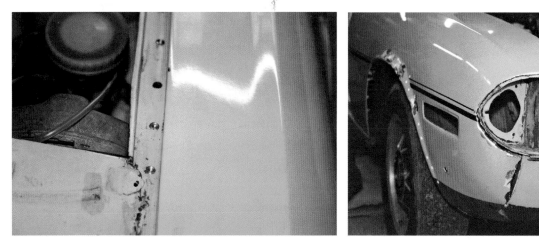
4-1g. ... and valance seam.

4-1e. Slit around lamp ...

4-1h. Cut front deck seam ...

4-1f. ... and engine bay ...

4-1i. ... wing is now free.

Wing replacement is essentially a job which can be performed in isolation, but be warned, removing wings on older cars will often reveal further work to be done, and skimping on this work will cost you in the long run. This is largely true of all panels, of course.

It's a good idea to familiarise yourself with the structure of your car before you start removing panels, since you may not have the line of the supporting pieces to work to if they fall off with the panel you are replacing. This may sound obvious, but it's all too easy to get carried away

with knocking off bits of rust and filler, only to find that what you've got left is of little help when it comes to reassembly. A bit of forethought will go a long way, and working on one side of the car at a time will leave you with a reference. Also, seeking advice from people who

4-1j. *Sans* wing.

4-1k. Lift off waste metal.

have done the job already can never be underestimated, and clubs, magazines and fellow owners can save you a lot of grief.

For example, look at the rear edge of the mini wing – it's curved to match the scuttle. The obvious thing to do is close the panels together, mate the curves and align the wing to the adjacent front and A-post panels. The trouble is that if you do this, the wings will be a few millimetres back, and the bonnet will never close. I've had to rescue several cars from this predicament, which was simply the result of over-enthusiastic owners getting ahead of themselves.

A REAL-LIFE EXAMPLE
The Triumph Stag illustrates the issues we're dealing with very well; the panels are large, with even gaps, and they require a variety of techniques.

Along with your usual tools you will need: an angle grinder with cutting, grinding and fibre discs; a hammer and dolly; as many welding clamps as you can get; 1/8in pop rivets and a riveter (or pan head PKs); a drill with 1/8in bits; a spot weld drill; a 3M Clean 'n Strip wheel, or similar; axle stands and a trolley jack; and, of course, welding gear – preferably MIG and spot. Needless to say, you should also have all the relevant safety gear.

Like those on most cars, Stag wings are prone to damage from water, stone chipping and accidents. Unusually, though, Stag wings have an inner arch, which increases the likelihood of rot and adds to the difficulty of the job. The front valance and front deck seams (between the bonnet and the lamps), are concealed, which gives us a clue to the original build order.

These parts – the wings, front deck and valance – are joined and pulled back over and onto the inner wings, wheelarches and lamp panels. To do this a gap is left in front of the inner arch which is filled with a fillet piece, and a gap is left which allows road spray to be blasted into the space behind the wing.

As with many cars, the Stag's sills continue behind the wing. I've dealt with a lot of cars, though, on which only the exposed part of the the the sills has been replaced. This is unacceptable, of course, and in many cases dangerous. Again, familiarise yourself with your vehicle's structure before committing yourself.

Having assessed the job, the first thing to do is to strip it. First, remove as much as you can from the repair area. In this case, that means door, sill trim, lights and bumper. Don't remove the bonnet at this stage, though, as it will help with the alignment, although the bonnet stay guide (a small piece attached to the inner wing) is in the way, and not worth saving if doing the nearside wing. Replace the wing and fit a new bonnet stay after. Wings are often replaced in pairs, of course, but don't remove the valance at the same time, as this will allow the lamp panel to collapse under the weight of the bonnet.

The door is easier to handle if it's stripped out first. Also, note that any door which is bolted to the hinge and, in turn, to the post, is best removed leaving the hinge in situ.

Protect your windscreen with card or sheeting, and cover your trim; it's time to start work.

Reveal the spot welds (you'll find them along the top and door-shut edges, as well as around the lamps), with a bit of emery or with the 3M wheel, and then drill them out with your cobalt drill. You'll also find spot welds under the A-post and wheelarch, but these are often too corroded to drill (try anyway).

You may have noticed that I've not said to set the car on stands as yet. Obviously you can't drill under the wheelarch whilst the car's on the floor, but,

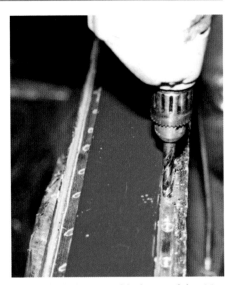

4-2b. Drilling spot weld – be careful not to hole-through.

with a Stag, you can't align anything with the car raised as it is prone to 'beaming' (a form of structural distortion – bowing along the length). The only answer is a lot of fiddling about with a jack ... Sorry.

The next job is to split around the panel, starting along the top edge, then work along the inner edge of the welded flange (see picture 4-1e) leaving the row of drilled spot welds attached to the flitch plate (inner wing). Do the same around the lamps and door edge. Cutting around the arch is a bit trickier, however, as the inner arch is a bit close for comfort, but you can cut high to avoid it, or go close and run your chisel over the inner metal. **Note!** Always remember that you want to avoid moving any of the structures that will remain.

Next, using the cutting disc, cut on the wing side of the top deck seam and then down the valance seam. If the valance is not going to be replaced, cut on the wing side. If the valance is going, however, feel free to hack it, but remember that leaving it in place can help with wing alignment.

4-2a. Revealing spot welds with abrasive wheel.

4-3a. Cutting with grinder – use only correct disk.

4-3b. Cutting with hacksaw – only where access allows.

4-5. Remnants of seam. Do not try to lift the waste edge by hand as it is very sharp!

4-6. Locate new panel. Note the mark made before removal of old metal.

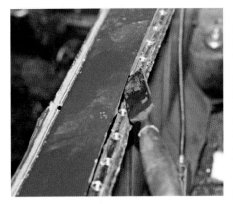

4-3c. Cutting with the chisel – make sure you keep the tool sharp.

Although the chisel and the cutting disc are pretty much interchangeable, to my mind the grinder lacks finesse, but that's a quality some people like!

If all has gone to plan, your wing will now be free. If it isn't, unpick it as required, using tin-snips, hacksaw, etc, and lift your rotten old wing clear (while wearing gloves, of course).

The previously concealed welds can now be drilled out and, along with the rest of the gash metal, the seams can be unpicked. Use your chisel to lift the edge and peel off the waste with a good self-grip wrench or a pair of swan-neck pliers. Any welds you might have missed can be drilled, or you can 'wiggle' them off. This is preferable to ripping them out.

When the remains of the old panel have been removed, you must clean the mounting surfaces with a grinder (use a soft 36 grit disc or a hard grinding disc, and don't be tempted to use the thinner, cutting disc, as damage to yourself and your car is quite likely).

The next step is to use a bumping hammer and a flat dolly to realign any metal you have disrupted, or you'll struggle to get a close fit. Do not underestimate the importance of this process (known as tapping-up), and take the time to do it properly.

DRILLING SPOT WELDS
If your spot welds prove hard to locate, you may find that a light stroke of the soft disc of your grinder might help. If that doesn't help, try burning off the paint, or remove it with a nylon abrasive disc on your drill. Note, though, that a short length of weld seam can give off a disproportionate amount of paint dust.

A properly closed spot weld should be drilled squarely into the centre to a depth of half the total metal, which is to say the thickness of the panel you hope to remove. You will get a feel for this, and don't worry if you hole-through – it happens. Occasionally, you will encounter poorly formed spot welds where the electrodes have failed to close to the same point. In these cases the centre of the weld will be raised and pitched at an angle to the seam. These welds can be difficult to drill, as it's tricky to locate and accurately drill the point of attachment. One solution is to use an oversized drill bit; another is to use a smaller bit and drill several times.

'Wiggle' off the waste metal using a pair of mole-type self-grip pliers. Start by lifting the end of the waste edge square and grip firmly with your pliers. Rather than ripping off the weld, try to stress-fracture the metal immediately around the weld centre by gently wiggling the pliers in a circular motion, before lifting sharply. This works because the metal you are trying to break is softer then the weld itself.

An alternative method is to cut the waste metal on each side of a weld, lift each piece until they close and wiggle them as one. You should now be left with the weld centre standing proud of the substrate. This must be cleaned with the grinder to give a level base for the new panel. There's always the risk that the weld will fracture on the wrong side, leaving you with a hole in the substrate. This will act as a water trap if not sealed.

4-4. Lift off panel – for safety ensure you are wearing gloves.

Chapter 5
Basic panel fitment

I will now show how the Stag wing is replaced. For the sake of clarity, I'll overlook the problems that had to be dealt with behind the wing, and move straight on to the re-attachment process.

The quickest, easiest, and more original way to do the job is to use a spot welder. You must always remember, though, that, in order to get a good weld, you must clean off all the paint on both sides of any joint. The Clean 'n' Strip wheel comes into its own here, and a coat of spray zinc is also a good idea.

If you're just using a MIG welder, then you'll have to drill or hole-punch along the welding seam, and, of course, grind off any excess afterwards.

ALIGNMENT
With the bonnet open, sit the new wing in place and check the curve of the scuttle and the scallop on the front to get your fore and aft positions. Clamp the wing in place inside the engine bay, then drill and pop rivet (or PK) the wing in place. If, after checking, the fit is not correct, the holes will at least give you a datum to work from. The use of pop rivets allows you to lower the bonnet and check for an even gap on both sides, as well as along the front and rear edges. Only when you're completely happy with the fit should you worry about the door gap. Initially, a single clamp below the sill will suffice to hold the wing in place. Refit the door using two bolts per hinge and the paint marks as a guide.

You'll notice that pushing the rear section of the wing inward will tend to move it upward. This will affect the dog-leg and swage line level. After a few minutes' tinkering, you can remove the door and 'pop' the wing edge in place.

Re-refit the door and check again (this can get very tiresome). When the door gap is all tidy, move forward and clamp around the lights, down inside the valance seam, and around the wheelarch.

Note! Cars with inner wheelarches offer very little scope for adjustment if the arch is intact. So, during the alignment process, be prepared to remove the wing so as to nip out a bit of shrapnel or dress a seam. Your patience and exactitude will pay off in the long run.

If, whilst aligning a panel or group of panels, you find things not adding up, which is often the case, bear in mind that your car has a history, and it's likely something has been replaced or repaired at some point. Always try to work to what you know to be true. This may mean that, in order to set up the wing, you'll have to work to the scuttle and rear quarter panel, which in turn means reassessing the fit of the door and the bonnet.

Remember that your wing must be correct in all planes. Many car doors open around the trailing edge of the wing, for example, and will foul if the wing is proud.

WELDING AT LAST
I always start by welding along the top

edge. Don't forget that, if you're using a MIG welder, you will need to drill holes. I use a spot welder where I can, which effectively means just the top, lamp, and door shut seams. Don't forget the three little blobs of weld on the turret.

Next, I secure the front and rear of the deck panel with a MIG weld. **Note!** I generally use overlapping MIG/spot for this joint, and fake the seam with filler. Some owners prefer braze, of course (each to his own), but the original joint is impossible. How you weld the valance seam is also a matter of choice. You could, of course, break your wrist and weld it from the inside, though I prefer to weld into the joint and grind it off carefully, then fake the seam (this actually works quite well).

Any temporary fixings such as PKs and pop rivets must be removed and the holes welded up (or you will have holes that shouldn't be there!). In order to make the wing sit flat relative to the door and sill, the bottom of the door seam must be pushed in and fixed with weld to the top of the sill.

Now comes the nasty bit: the wheelarch. Even if you have a spot welder, it's unlikely that you'll have the proper electrodes for this part of the job, so drilling and plug welding is the order of the day. Clamp the arches together as you work your way round. If you find yourself clamping onto a visible area, interpose a filler spreader to save marking the paint.

Note! Wear a visor when drilling the

wheelarch; that swarf is evil and it's also a certainty that welding overhead will mean falling drops of molten metal, so watch out, and tape up your sleeves!

WELDING COMPLETED

All that remains now is to grind off and prepare for painting. The secret of grinding off is simply to watch carefully and take your time, 'stroke' rather than 'jab.' Start with a hard disc and finish off with a 36 grit soft.

The only filler you should require is on the top deck (which always distorts), on the valance seam (depending, of course, on how you approached it), and possibly under the wheelarch, around the welds. A coat of zinc or red oxide on the seams is worth considering, but check with whomever is going to paint it first.

PROBLEM AREAS

Take a careful look at the A-post dog-leg. If it's blistered, you might be able to displace the rusted and pin-holed metal with MIG

weld (see picture 5-1a). More extensive rot will require new bits of metal being let in. Don't be tempted to plug it over, as the rot will only come back worse than ever. Knocking off the gutter will help to clarify things. Do this by removing the rivets and striking into the lower outside corner with a chisel or bolster. Clean up with a soft disc on the grinder, and rust proof with a good sealer before re-closing. New gutters are cheap, and fit OK (ish), though I prefer to re-use the originals with fresh metal where needed.

Because the sills are the most important structural member on the car, they must be checked thoroughly. Localised rot behind

the wing can legitimately be patched, though, with a bit of care.

The state of the inner wheelarch can usually be assessed by running your fingers around it, but anyone can be caught out. I've seen wheelarches made of filler, with not a weld in sight, which I took to be sound.

5-1b. Essential inner arch repair. Make good as required.

5-1c. Zinc weld areas to prevent rust and promote electrical conductivity.

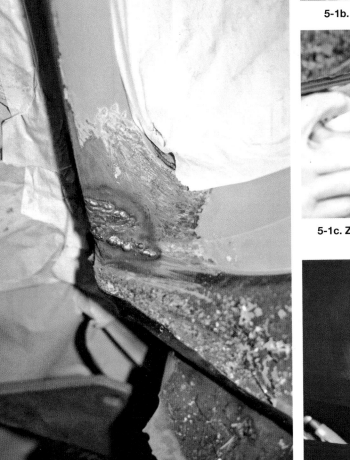

5-1a. Do the minor repair to the dog-leg now.

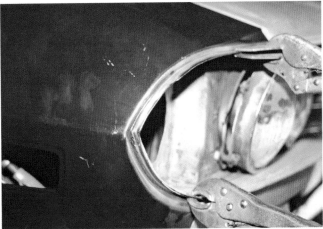

5-1d. Pay close attention to alignment; front ...

5-1e. ... and bonnet line ...

5-1g. Welding complete. The car is prepared for the paintshop.

5-1f. ... and rear.

5-1h. Job done and the car is returned to its owner.

Here's a great tip: make up repair sections by folding two inch wide strips of 20swg steel into an L-section. Then, with a cross pien hammer, strike at right angles to the length along one face. This will cause the hammered face to spread and the other face to curve into an arc. With practice, this technique, known as 'edge spreading,' is invaluable for situations like this when you need a curved repair section. This is shown in detail later. Complete inner wheelarches and repair sections are available, of course, as are splash panel/sill closures. However, bear in mind that fitment of any repairs to the inner wheelarch must be double-checked with the wing in its final location.

As you must have gathered by now, fitting a wing is not so simple a job as some would have you believe. There are many considerations and even more pitfalls. However, if you think twice before you act at every stage, you can turn out a job to be proud of.

Chapter 6
Sectional repairs to basic panels

Whether it's originality, necessity, or financial constraint that motivates you to salvage rather than replace your rotten panel, you always have options. Bottoms are available for most popular models, as are wheelarches and, occasionally, headlamp sections, and what you can't buy you can often make. Alternatively, two rotten wings, for example, can be cobbled together to make one perfect item.

CIRCULAR PATCHES
This technique has its roots in boiler making and was originally used in conjunction with gas welding. MIG does pretty well, though, and I've saved many panels this way.

The rationale behind using this shape for the patch is based on the behaviour of the metal during welding. A disc will expand and contract more evenly than a piece with corners. The down side, however, is that the hole is harder to cut out, but it is worth the effort if you want a quality job.

The first step is to decide how much needs to be replaced. As this method is usually reserved for mid-panel rot which has eaten through from the inside, it's unwise to make assumptions regarding the extent of the rot based on what you can see from the outside.

Once you've decided upon the extent of the problem, mark out a circle on the panel using a pair of dividers, and transfer this to a piece of 20 swg. Next, cut out the

new piece and shape it to fit (traditionally, this piece is rolled to break the surface tension before contouring). Obviously, the exact shaping is different for each job. Here are two examples: pics 6-1a to 6-1j show a simple circular patch, pics 6-2a to 6-2l – tricky!

6-1a to 6-1j. A simple circular patch.

6-1a. The size of the patch is critical.

6-1b. Drill with care.

6-1c. Cut with care.

6-1d. Removal of gash metal.

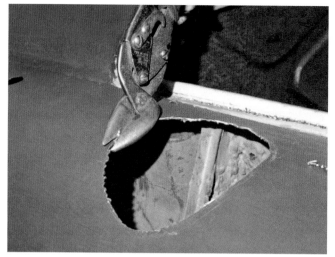

6-1e. Clean up hole.

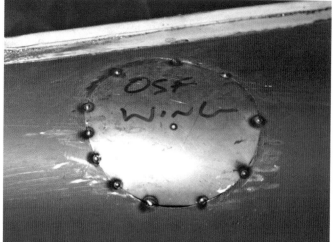

6-1h. Careful tacking.

6-1f. Tidy up any distortion.

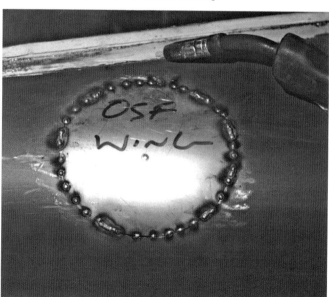

6-1i. Take time with welding.

6-1g. Align new piece – note temporary handle.

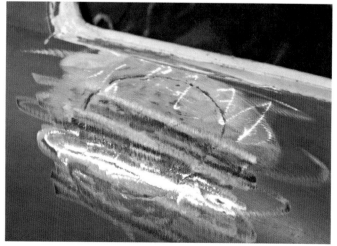

6-1j. After grinding the repair looks good.

6-2a to 6-2l. Complex circular patch.

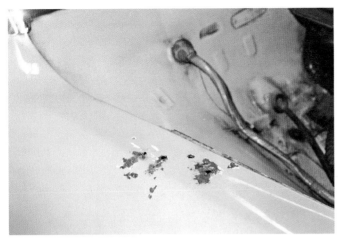

6-2a. The location of the rot demands a more complex repair.

6-2d. New metal shaped to fit.

6-2b. Disk and damage revealed.

6-2e. Tape to mark hole.

6-2c. Tape and mark folds.

6-2f. Cutting out gash metal.

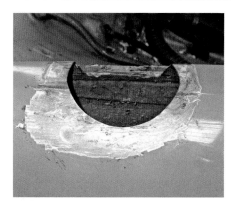

6-2g. Tidy up.

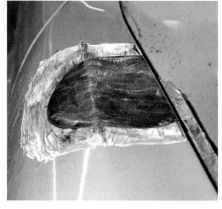

6-2h. New metal in place.

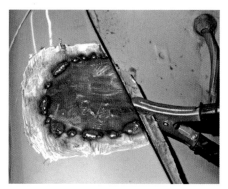

6-2i. Careful tacking.

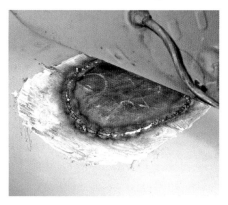

6-2j. Welding complete.

6-2l. The wing is made good at a fraction of the price of a new one!

6-2k. Not bad, eh?

Hold the new section in situ and tack it level (a wire handle is handy – see pic 6-1g). Intergrip clamps could also be used for this.

Space the consecutive tacks as far apart as possible so as to dissipate the heat evenly. It's critical that the panels be exactly flush at each point of weld, so take your time and, if necessary, dress lightly with hammer and dolly. Continue the tacks until they are $1/2$in or so apart.

Once you begin to run out of space for tack welds, you have to fill in the gaps. Again, rather than stitches, I find overlapping spots will distort less.

Once the welding is finished, clean off the excess weld with a hard disc on your angle grinder, then finish off with a 36grt soft disc. Don't press too hard, of course, and stroke rather than dig at it.

Corner repair section

This is the same job but with corners, shown in pictures 6-3a to 6-3c being put to good use on a door skin. This technique is a must for Triumph Herald rear quarter panels, fore and aft of the wheelarch. The work sequence is just as before, though you'll probably find it easier to do a dry run with a card template, before making the metal piece which you can then scribe around for the cut line. **Note!** For door skin repairs, don't fold the return edge until after the welding has been completed, so as to preserve the surface tension.

6-3a to 6-3c. Corner repair patch.

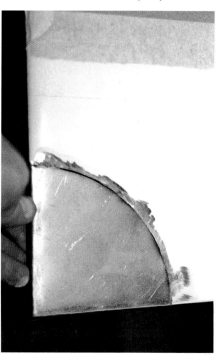

6-3a. Corner repair patch used on door skin.

The Ford Anglia repair is probably at the more fiddly end of the scale, but new wings, if I could find them, are £700 each, which is £650 more than the car is worth! The repair to the Jaguar was fairly straightforward by comparison.

When you are completely happy with the patch, mark its location with tape or pencil and scribe closely around it onto the panel.

The next step involves cutting out the gash metal, and the best method for this is probably to drill a series of holes inside the circle and to then nip between them with snips, chisel, and grinder, before cleaning up with a half round file. Take care not to distort the panel, of course, and don't go outside of the line.

6-3b. It must be a good fit.

6-4a to 6-4c Sill end.

6-4a. New piece made ready.

6-4c. It needs just a skim of filler.

6-4b. The new piece is put into place.

SALVAGED PANEL SECTIONS

The best way to ensure you get an accurate repair section, of course, is to cut one off another car.

The Jaguar scuttle piece you see pictured would have been a bit fiddly to make, but luckily the owner had another dead car. This was a very straightforward job, but required a very close fit to keep the gap correct around the vent flap. I went for a square cut, which I know goes against what I've advised up until now, but time was against me. I trial-fitted the vent flap before committing myself to weld. A stepped (joddled) lap-joint can be employed in situations like this, since the overlap allows for some final adjustment before welding, and lessens the risk of burning through.

6-3c. Dress flange around after welding.

Sill end

This Stag sill was perfect apart from this rotten end and some superficial pitting, so complete replacement was not necessary. The patch may look pretty square, but the curve of the panel will help to control the distortion. This piece was made using a template taken from the other side of the car. As you can see, I've had to 'petal' the rear edge to get the compound curve. I would have used a lap joint, for greater strength and flexibility of alignment, had the join not been so close to the end of the sill.

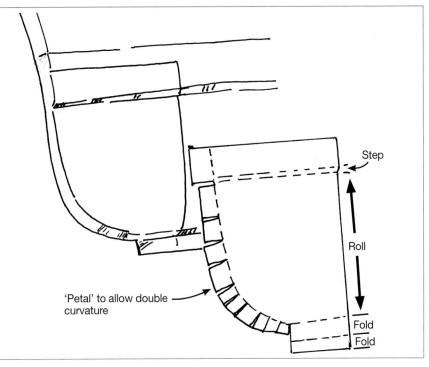

'Petal' to allow double curvature

Step

Roll

Fold

Fold

Sill end.

6-5a & 6-5b. Use of salvaged parts – screen surround top.

6-6a & 6-6b. Jag scuttle repair, use of salvaged parts.

6-5a. The joint must be accurate ...

6-6a. Rotten area of scuttle is carefully removed using a cutting disk ...

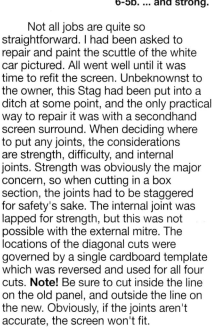

6-5b. ... and strong.

6-6b. ... and accurately positioned before welding.

Not all jobs are quite so straightforward. I had been asked to repair and paint the scuttle of the white car pictured. All went well until it was time to refit the screen. Unbeknownst to the owner, this Stag had been put into a ditch at some point, and the only practical way to repair it was with a secondhand screen surround. When deciding where to put any joints, the considerations are strength, difficulty, and internal joints. Strength was obviously the major concern, so when cutting in a box section, the joints had to be staggered for safety's sake. The internal joint was lapped for strength, but this was not possible with the external mitre. The locations of the diagonal cuts were governed by a single cardboard template which was reversed and used for all four cuts. **Note!** Be sure to cut inside the line on the old panel, and outside the line on the new. Obviously, if the joints aren't accurate, the screen won't fit.

TYPICAL LOWER WING SECTIONAL REPAIR

This is a typical wing from the last century, now in need of rectification. Start by deciding how much to replace, and cut the template card to suit. Then, using a ruler or straight edge to guide you, score a line for the bottom edge. Next, set the back edge, and then establish a top line, both of which must be clearly marked and adhered to. It's often a good idea to decide the depth from the start, and then define it with tape on the panel (for without a datum, you **will** fudge the job). If you find the template wandering, stick it along the top edge. The front edge is the fiddly bit, so take care.

6-7a to 6-7j. Fabricate and fit lower wing section.

6-7a.

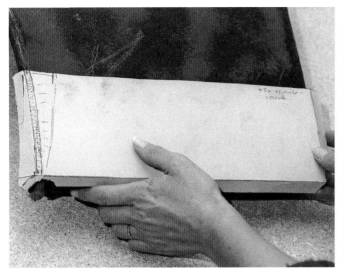

6-7b.

6-7e.

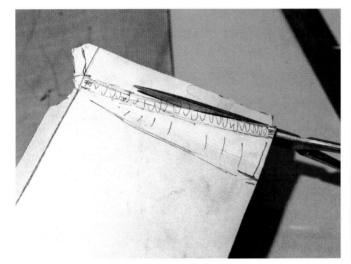

6-7c.

6-7f.

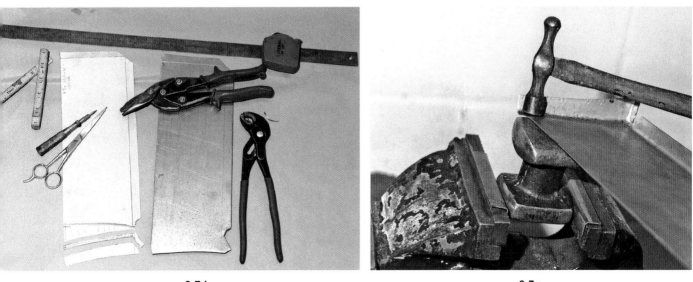

6-7d.

6-7g.

6-7h.

6-7i.

6-7j.

Work the card over with your thumbs, and mark off the differing radii, along with areas for shrinkage, stretch and deformation. Having completed the main template, make as many contour templates as you see fit. Use these to form and fit the new piece correctly.

With all the information transcribed, the new piece is cut out exactly. You must now decide on a work order, so as not to end up having to undo previous good work. You can't fold a curve, and you can't curve a fold you know, as someone once said!

The first step is to break the surface tension and impart a slight curve to the piece (I passed the metal through the roller, though a mallet and pipe would have

done – the mallet will give shape without stretching). The next step is to break the rear edge in the vice, perhaps using a urethane mallet to control the fold. Now, the trickier front edge, with its various radii (I started to form the wheelarch area with pliers, as this gave more precision, then, holding the arch lip in the vice, I tapped gingerly around it). So small an area of grip means lots of repositioning but also greater control.

The new section is starting to look like something now and needs only the flaring behind the arch. By comparing the horizontal template to the dollies, it's easy to find the correct one for the job. After setting the dolly in the vice and marking up inside the piece from the original template, work the area to be raised with a very light hammer. All that remains now is to weld it on.

Since the wing was actually off the car, I opted for spotting with butt welds where the lap would show. Accurate cutting is critical if this is going to appear seamless, though, and a neatly joddled edge will be of great help. Continued use of templates during assembly saves time and hassle.

PROPRIETARY WING BOTTOM SECTION

It is possible to purchase a new wing bottom, of course, and fitting it should be pretty easy. However, I can tell you that many wing sections do not fit brilliantly, and require as much tinkering to make them fit as is needed to fabricate a piece from scratch. Assuming your new section to be true, it's down to you to fit it accurately, and templates taken before removal of the old section can save you

6-8b.

a lot of time. If you're working with the wing on the car, use of joddled main seam and MIG plug welds will suffice, though most tin bashers would prefer to put a continuous seam of overlapping MIG spots (best achieved by first tacking along the hollow which forms between the top of the new piece and the joddled step). For the front and rear edges, though, you'll need a short section of butt joint so as not to show the extra thickness of metal.

The example shown here had the wing opened in order to replace the sill, a section of inner wheelarch was required before fitting. See Shrinking and Stretching.

PROPRIETARY BOOT LID SECTION

The Jaguar boot lid repair section shown here was acquired through the owners' club and is a nicely made piece. In order to locate the new section I had the choice of either lipping the new metal over the old, and then scribing a line, or measuring the

6-8a & 6-8b. Proprietary wing bottom and internal repair.

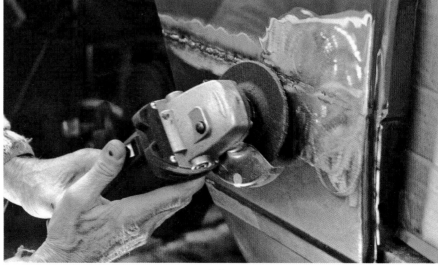

6-8a.

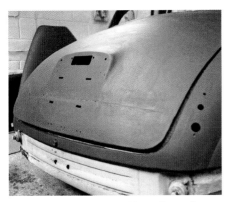

6-9. Proprietary boot lid repair section.

6-10a to 6-10d. Repair to supporting structure.

6-10a.

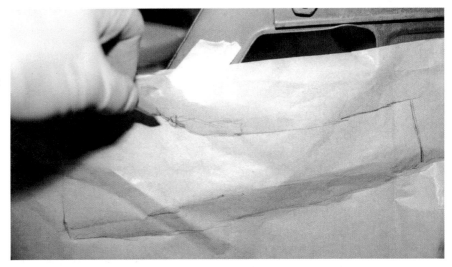

6-10b.

6-10c.

depth of the new piece and transcribing the line with a flexible steel rule. Both methods require that the waste metal be removed before the new section can be positioned for a final marking of the joint line. The bottom edge of the repair had to be dressed, 'door skin' fashion, over the frame (see the section on doors), and only when this was done could the boot be closed to check the line of the aperture.

I had to use joddled lap-MIG welding, since the access didn't permit the use of the spot welder, and a small section of butt joint was needed at each end to allow for a flush fit. With a little care, heat distortion should not be a problem on panels such as this, since they curve in all planes. The same joint on a flat panel, however, might have incurred a great deal more distortion.

The elongated holes hold the numberplate plinth, so it was in my best interests to double-check that this fitted before committing the new metal in place.

SUPPORTING STRUCTURES & ALIGNMENT

The lower section of this inner rear quarter panel needed to be replaced before the rear wing and boot floor could be repaired. A simple paper template was employed, along with a little bit of educated guesswork. This job is detailed more fully in the section on rear wings. Due to the poor state of the panel, I couldn't finish the lower edge until after the new outer panel was in place.

Section upon section

It's quite common to make up one piece and then find that the panel it joins to is also rotten. The accompanying pictures show the trouble with owning a soft top in Britain; rain passing into the rear quarter panels has eaten away inside the B-post foot, and eventually into the sill itself. This car was structurally unsound, and needed serious attention. However, a new sill B-post foot and rear wing would have cost thousands of pounds to buy, fit and paint. Structural integrity aside, you can't

6-10d.

just wade into a job like this with a grinder and hope to sew it up again neatly. What's needed is a plan of action. Remember that once a piece has been cut out, it is no longer there to be worked to. You'll have to make up the pieces, or at least their patterns, in the reverse order to their final fitment. I've done enough of these cars to have a good idea of what's waiting behind a panel, so I knew that, in this case, making and locating a new rear quarter panel section was imperative before I chopped out any of the sill.

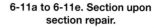

6-11a to 6-11e. Section upon section repair.

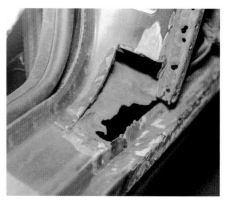

6-11a.

6-11b.

6-11c.

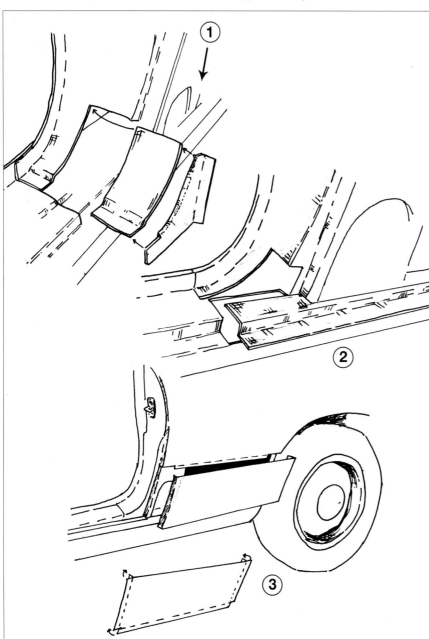

Sectional repairs. 1. B-post foot is made in two pieces, turned over top of outer. Allow hotter weld. 2. Folds in sill provide location. 3. Welding flat section is prone to distortion/door shut is critical.

6-11d.

6-11e.

The rear quarter panel section is basically a flat panel, and is, therefore, a 'major' distortion area. The size of the repair section is governed by the extent of the damage, of course, and the amount of access needed to effect proper sill repairs. The repair section is initially created using a paper template, and then the top edge is joddled and lapped, the front and rear are folded and spot welded, and the bottom edge is attached to the sill by overlapping spots of MIG. Top and bottom must be welded with great care to avoid an excess of pug. **Note!** In the case of larger sections, the front edge should be gently curved by edge shrinking.

The B-post foot is fabricated from two pieces, each made using its own template. To join the pieces on the reverse curve, I left a 1/8in lip which was turned over on the inside.

The sill repair section is a simple step-folded piece in 18 gauge, since both strength and accurate location are issues when it comes to sill repairs.

BOWL SECTIONS

The lower rear wing section shown in the accompanying pictures is curved behind the wheelarch, but runs into a bowl section toward the rear of the car. This is something of an impossible shape, however, as it cannot be made without removing some metal, while at the same time stretching (by means of planishing), the material in the bowl area. I found that the best way to fabricate such a piece is to

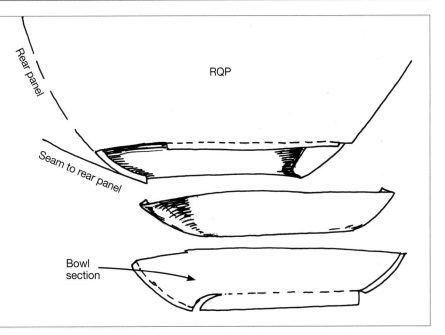

Sectional repairs. This piece incorporated both curves and bowled areas.

6-12. Bowl section repair.

start with a paper template taken from the other side of the car. When the template is cut and wrapped around the replacement panel, you'll be able to see where the metal needs to be lost.

Welding is best carried out by lap joint in the areas that permit it, and butt joints for the more curved areas. Although the curve of the panel should help to control the distortion, it's always a good idea to keep consecutive tacks apart when welding.

PILLAR JOINTS

From time to time the need arises for joints to be put in areas that run into sills and posts. The detail here is the front top of a door skin and clearly shows the issues you will face.

The front of the joint has some tricky swaging which requires very close matching and precise welding. There is little room for filler after the excess weld has been removed. Any misregister or lumpiness would ruin the door shut line.

The flat area accommodates a mirror. While this allows for less tidy welding, any excess might prevent the mirror from sitting flush.

I'd tend to employ lap joints in cases where strength is an issue, though, of course, a simple lap is not possible in areas that have a lot of folds and swages. The way around this problem would be to split any sharp edges and form a step with the edge set on the flats. The end result should be a strong and accurate joint. The other advantage of this type

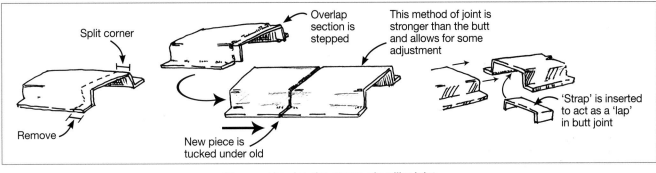

Diagram showing the stages of a pillar joint.

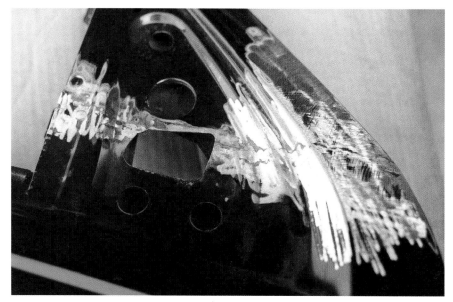

6-13. Pillar joint.

of joint is that it allows for a degree of adjustment.

METHODS OF JOINING & FIXING

The MIG welder became the mainstay of the commercial bodyshop during the 1980s, and tended to replace oxyacetylene. Toward the end of the 1990s, however, a move to replace the MIG in some applications was instigated by insurance companies. It was argued that the MIG welds were too tough and didn't 'give' in the controlled manner required by the designer. A new generation of single-sided spot welders then came to the fore. Now, though, in the early part of the twenty-first century, the all-aluminium vehicle is presenting a new set of welding challenges.

It's still the case, though, that for the home restorer and small bodyshop, the MIG remains central. My own current set-up consists of a small, 150 amp Cebora on a home-made trolley (with a Y size cylinder), along with a hand-operated resistance spot welder.

Some purists, of course, regard gas welding as more 'authentic,' and so have an increased range of possible techniques.

Gas welding

Gas welding, either by pure fusion of the panels or with a filler rod, offers all of the joint configurations possible with MIG, but with less cleaning up required. The down side is the potential for greater distortion, of course, and the obvious risks posed by a flame and two bottles of explosive gas.

Brazing and bronze welding have been used extensively in the manufacture and repair of vehicles over the years.

Brazing is akin to soldering, of course, in that a filler material (nominally brass), is used to join the panels. The metal being joined doesn't reach a high enough temperature to melt, though, so no actual fusion takes place. In bronze welding, on the other hand, the base metal is brought up to a tinning temperature (usually red), and the joint produced is stronger. The terms brazing and bronze welding are not, therefore, interchangeable. These two techniques have gone out of vogue in recent years, possibly due to an association with what is regarded as 'bodging.' In Britain, for example, braze or bronze weld are not regarded as acceptable for chassis repairs, which seems to be somewhat shortsighted to me, as good braze will be stronger than a poor weld. Both brazing and bronze welding rely on a good deal of surface contact, and a closeness of fit to ensure capillary action.

Soldering

Soft solder, due to its low melting point, is handy for temporarily fixing handles onto panels before pulling. Its use of capillary action also makes it handy for the repair of (purged!) petrol tanks and water vessels. Many brackets and minor parts made of brass will require soft soldering for their repair.

Although silver soldering (or silver brazing), was originally a jewellery technique, it has evolved into an important part of modern vehicle manufacture, and may be of use to you. Silver solder offers a compromise between soft solder and welding. Silver soldering is carried out with an oxyacetylene torch and is useful for applications where fusion welding would

seriously distort the base metal. Very light gauge brass, stainless or mild steel sheet, along with components made from nickel, bronze and copper, can be joined effectively with this technique.

Aluminium brazing, which is often confused with 'aluminium welding,' uses an alloy of aluminium as a filler material, but which has a much lower melting point than the parent metal. The effectiveness and viability of this technique depends on the composition of the parent metal. Alloys consisting of more than 2 per cent magnesium, for example, will not generally work well as the oxide film is difficult to remove with standard fluxes. Other alloys will not be suitable due to low melting points.

Chemical bonding

For as long as I can remember, the promise of panel adhesives has been on the horizon. In the mid 1980s, for example, at least two companies brought out bonding systems which claimed to be suitable for fixing metal panels in place. Having used them both once, and once only, I think we can safely say that their day has not yet come.

Isocyanate/polyurethane flexible bonding sealer is an enormously strong adhesive, however, which draws moisture out of a joint as it cures. This product, despite not being very original, has many uses in classic car restoration.

Cold rivets

Cold rivets resemble short, blunt nails, and are usually worked with a hammer and one or two rivet 'sets.' A set is first used to pass the rivet through the pre-drilled holes in the workpiece, and a second set is used to close the pieces together. With the rivet head supported by one set, the shaft is worked to form another head on the other side by use of a hammer directly, or by beating the second set. Cold rivets can be of steel, copper, brass or aluminium.

Pop rivets

The pop rivet or 'blind' rivet dates back to the 1930s and is an innovation of the aeroplane industry. The term blind refers its suitability for jobs where only one side is accessible. Nowadays, pop rivets come in a huge number of varieties. Many sizes, lengths and specialised applications are catered for, including 'bifurcated' designs which apply little or no outward pressure against the hole. Many trims and minor brackets and the like are fixed with blind rivets, which may be of steel or aluminium. Pop rivets are the ideal temporary fixing, as the head offers little interference in doorways and shut lines, and they can be quickly removed by drilling. Consult your local fixings supplier for the range available.

Chapter 7
Doors

Because of their very nature, car door skins are prone to rusting. Water will always pass the weather strip, for example, and, if it can't drain, will pool along the bottom edge and creep into the seams. Accident damage is also very common, of course. Water will also sit behind and under the door, allowing rust to attack the frame from both sides if the paint has been breached in any way. Trims, too, will hold moisture and dirt, as will rubber seals. It's no wonder, therefore, that you poor old motor is in less than pristine condition in the entrance department. Many classics have, of course, been bodged up in this area, so don't be too surprised to find large gobs of filler and newsprint when you start to unpick what you took to be good metal.

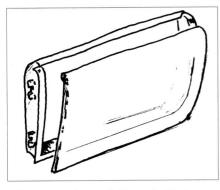

Door is made up of skin mated to inner shell.

DOOR CONSTRUCTION
All doors are basically made up from two panels: the outer panel or skin, and the inner structure. These two items are joined along the front, rear and bottom edges by means of a return edge on the skin, which is turned over and folded onto a mounting flange. The top edge of the door body is usually open, of course, and accommodates the glass with its framework and/or runners. Window frames are either welded or bolted onto the inner door panel. Some models have frames which raise and lower with the window itself, of course, while others, such as the later Triumph Spitfires, have no frame to speak of, relying instead on the runners and winder mechanism to support and locate the side glass.

Most car doors are fairly heavy structures when fully fitted, and usually need pretty substantial hinges and reinforcement around the front face. This reinforcement could take the form of simple load-spreading plates or, perhaps, an internal box section. Additionally, the design of the hinge may dictate internal captive nut plates or similar fiddly details.

Although few classic vehicles feature side impact bars, as the term 'classic' expands to accommodate later models, this is something we'll have to consider. However, any vehicle which hoped to sell in the American market from the mid-seventies onward had to comply with safety regulations unheard of in Britain

at the time. One example of this is that Triumph Stags sold in the US had a double tubular bar welded into the doors, whereas the British model had nothing. The much-malignigned TR7, on the other hand, always came with a substantial box section beam through its waistline.

PROBLEM AREAS
Window frames
Because they are of a thicker gauge metal to the norm, and because they are positioned in such a way as to shed water rapidly, frames and runners tend to hold up pretty well. Points of attachment, though, are another matter, and often pose as water traps. Frame and runner sections are not easy things to make and, in truth, you may find replacement is a better and more economical solution (unless your vehicle is particularly rare, of course).

Hinges & supports
Corroded or damaged hinge areas pose two special problems for the restorer. Firstly, any repair must be strong enough to properly support the door and, secondly, the repair must not interfere with the alignment of the hinge, which has almost certainly moved by now. These two factors must be considered together, as they will compound each other. The best advice I can offer for now is to check twice before cutting or welding anything, and remember that the two hinges always have the same centre.

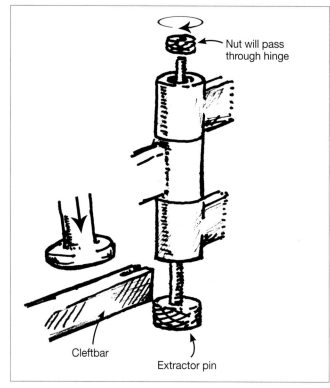

Nut will pass through hinge

Cleftbar

Extractor pin

Roll-pin extraction.

Hinge problems usually respond well to heat. Seized hinge pins or screws can be gently heated with a soft flame just enough to break the thin layer of rust which is holding them. If heat is not an option, however, then a good penetrating oil and a little patience goes a long way. Tight screws often let go after a little tapping with a hammer (through a well fitting driver). Whenever possible, when removing the door, leave the hinge where it is. Undoing the hinges at the A-post will usually make refitting the door a tad trickier. The opposite is often true for rear doors, however, since simply opening the front door may give you clear access to the B-post.

Check-strap
This is the device used to prevent the door from opening too far. Originally a simple leather or webbing strap, the check-strap has evolved over the years. Familiarise yourself with yours, and detach it before attempting to remove the door.

Removal & handling
The handiest thing to have around when handling car doors is an assistant. If you do employ the services of another pair of hands, though, it's imperative that one of you take charge and the other assist – this is not a democracy. Two people running the show will inevitably lead to damage and friction; trust me, I know.

Your assistant should take the weight and lift from the outside rear. The load can be reduced by stripping out the contents first, of course. You can now control the alignment from the inside front. Should you find yourself doing the job single-handedly, then my advice would be to crouch between the open door and the sill, and take the weight on one knee. Although many professionals employ this technique, the novice should only attempt it as a last resort.

Door bottoms
Door bottoms are often difficult to repair without disturbing the skin, since the rot usually extends to the mounting edge. Replacement sections are available for most popular classics, though the quality of fit is often less than precise. I prefer to fabricate my own repair sections, and will show you how it's done a bit later in the book. You should always enquire about the quality of parts before committing your hard-earned cash.

BASIC DOOR SKINNING PROCEDURE
To the novice restorer, reskinning a door may seem a rather daunting task. In truth, it is one of the easiest standalone jobs in the restoration process. In fact, as a trainee panel beater, skinning a door is probably the first real paid job you'd be given (it's profitable and not too tricky). If you learn nothing else from this book then your investment will have paid off.

Tools & equipment
• As well as a new panel, of course, you'll need an angle grinder with hard and soft grinding discs.
• A bench of some kind. My choice would be a 'Workmate,' with a 3ft x 2ft piece of carpeted ply clamped onto it.
• Bumping hammer and flat dolly. As a rule, the dolly should be approximately three times the weight of the hammer. Whereas I use a heavy cross pien for skinning, I know of others who advise the use of a light hammer with both round and square faces. You'll develop your own preferences as you become more proficient.
• Two or three mole clamps are ample, though it's a good idea to choose ones that will spread the pressure, so as not to mar the skin. Inserting filler spreaders or cardboard between clamp and skin will save a lot of filling later.
• A fine chisel. I use a carpenter's mortise chisel, as it gives a clean cut with good control.
• Welding gear. MIG equipment will cover you for any car, while the use of gas or a resistance spot welder will depend on how your particular door is put together.

7-1a to 7-1n. Door skinning.

7-1a.

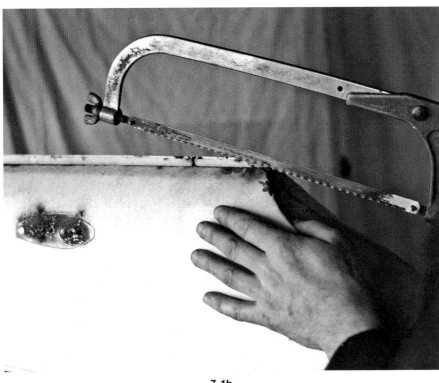

7-1b.

• You will, of course, have all the appropriate safety gear.

STARTING OFF
The first thing to do is to strip out the door and remove it from the car (preferably leaving the hinges behind). Lay the new skin over the old to get an idea of how it fits. You might also try the skin in the aperture, as this often reveals a lot about the quality of the panel. Be warned, though, the door skin edges can be sharp.

Grind off the return edge
As you can see, the edge of the skin is attached by a return edge wrapped over a lip on the door frame. Lay the door face down and, using your grinder square to the surface (with either a hard or a 36grt disc), grind through the outer layer of metal which connects the skin face to the return edge.

De-seam
Even after grinding, it's unlikely that the gash metal will simply fall off, so, with your sharp chisel angled slightly upward, and using some gentle persuasion from a hammer, split off the waste. A good pair of mole grips will come in handy here.

7-1c.

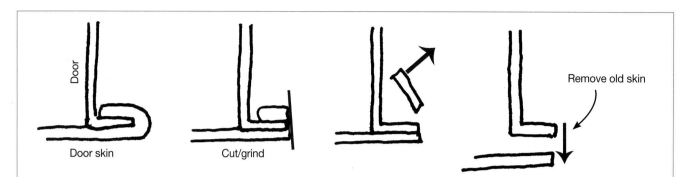

Door

Door skin

Cut/grind

Remove old skin

Removing an old door skin.

7-1d.

7-1f.

7-1e.

7-1g.

Caution! Don't be tempted to grab the gash metal with your hands, this stuff is like razor wire!

You may come across the odd spot weld on or under the waste edge. The easiest way to deal with these is to lift the gash strip on either side of the weld, cut it to within three inches or so, close to form a handle and then grip with the pliers. Now wiggle until the weld breaks. Dispose of this scrap metal with care, it really is very nasty.

How's your bottom?

If your door bottom is in need of some attention, now is the time to give it. Although you might think that this job would be easier at a later stage, you're much more likely to get it right if you do it now.

If the skin and the frame have started to part company, bring them back together with a couple of clamps, and lay the new bottom section over the old as best you can. Bear in mind that repair sections

for older cars tend to be hand-made, and generally require a bit of fettling. You can now trim the new piece to fit, but remember the true extent of the damage and the need to conceal your welding.

When the new piece is ready to fit, fix it tightly with clamps and/or self-tapping screws. Next, scribe a line around the new section, remove it again, and cut out the old metal to within half an inch or so of the line. Refit the new metal so you can get a more precise line for the critical joints where an overlap is possible. I'm sure you can see the benefit of leaving the old skin in situ to help with the location of the repair.

Remove the new piece (again), and make your final cuts. You could use butt joints all round, if your skills with a welder are up to it, of course, but lap joints would also be fine (except on the corners and mounting lip). You can employ a straight lap joint where the main joint is hidden by trim, but visible areas would best benefit from joddled (sunken) joints. If you don't have access to an edge set (joddler), don't worry; you can always tidy things up with a bit of filler when the job is done.

You can now weld in the repair if you wish, or you can wait until a bit later in order to gain better access.

Split off the skin

Turn the door so that it's face up. Insert your chisel and run it along the frame to part it from the skin (a few light taps with a hammer might be required). You may now be able to pull the skin up from its bottom edge by hand (wearing gloves, of course).

Any spot welds you find should be drilled out. It's also not uncommon to find the odd bit of brazing at the top of the door skin. This tends to be brittle, though, and should fracture if bent back on itself. Any remnants must then be ground off.

Clean up

Having discarded the old skin, you must now clean up the frame ready for the new one. Firstly, remove any old sealer with your chisel, then whiz over the mounting lip on both sides with your grinder or, better still, with a nylon abrasive wheel. Next, tap up the edge with your hammer and dolly to make good any damage caused during the previous steps. With the skin off, you may also now clean up the inside, along the line of the new bottom section, if you've not already attached it, that is.

Once the clean up is complete, weld in the new door bottom. Pay particular attention to its alignment along the mounting edge (in all planes), as any anomaly will show though the finished skin. If, like me, you're using an electric spot welder, then this is the best time to fix in any new piece. The down side is that, by not working with the old skin in situ, you have a greater chance of the door twisting

slightly. Keep the door supported evenly, and check the job in the door aperture before fixing the skin. Any minor twists can be tweaked out by setting the front on its hinges and then applying pressure to the rear top or bottom, as required.

Position the new skin

Working with the door face-up, sit the new skin on the frame and look for obvious points of location, such as swages and corners. Lightly clamp the skin into place, so as to check any areas that might cause problems (will the top lip-over if you start at the bottom, for example, or are the return edges too deep?). Although these sorts of difficulties are very minor if you

7-1i.

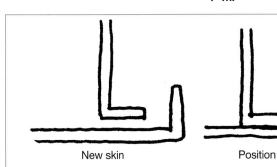

7-1h.

7-1j.

New skin   Position   Tap-up   Close

Fit new door skin.

address them now, they may become major headaches later if left unchecked.

From experience, I can tell you that the Stag skin featured here will fit best if it's tack welded at the very top, where it meets the guides for the window frame, and is then pulled down over the bottom edge of the frame.

Seal & clamp

Having decided on how best to fit the skin, but before any permanent fixing, remove the new panel one last time and set it safely aside. Brush a thin bead of sealer onto the closing face of the mounting lip, but don't allow this sealer to harden. Now, put the frame aside and place the skin face down on your (clean) bench. Next, position the door frame onto the skin and it clamp home, using spreaders or card to prevent marring, of course, and tack weld as required.

Tap up

Position the door so that one end overhangs the bench by about four inches (10cm). If you're right handed, hold your dolly in the palm of your left hand, with the flat face up. Take the hammer in your right hand and adopt a 'fighting stance,' with your knees slightly bent, left foot forward under your left hand.

If your door has a swage (feature) line, then that's the place to start tapping. If not, look for a break in the return edge or plump for the middle.

What you are aiming to do now is close the return edge over the lip, without stretching it, so don't attack it like a steam hammer, or try to punch it down with a single blow. It's best to let the weight of the hammer to do the work. Run up and down the edge, gradually flattening it after three or four passes. Keep your dolly flat against the skin, and don't allow it to bounce. Aim your hammer so as to strike the edge at about 45 degrees on the first pass, increasing the angle to 90 degrees on the third and any further passes. Use a cross pien for tight areas, or those areas behind a swage, but be careful not to stretch or misshape the surface of the skin.

As a general rule of thumb, work down each end from the middle, and then up. Finish along the bottom, unless your trial fit strongly suggests otherwise.

Fettle

What fettling (cleaning up), is required is really down to how well you've done the job.

Flip the door over and run your hand along the outer edge of the face. If it's a bit bumpy just flip it back and tap it up a bit tighter. Any clamp marks can be skimmed with filler.

When you're happy with the fit, and before filling or priming, a few tack welds are in order. One weld per corner, joining the skin to the frame, will surface to stop the door from distorting when in use.

7-1m.

7-1k.

7-1l.

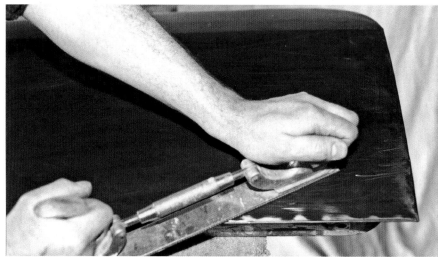

7-1n.

A FEW GOOD TIPS

• Don't allow your dolly to bounce. The dolly's job is to be your counter hold. Keep it firmly in place, and watch out for the line of the panel. Generally this means keeping the dolly parallel to the lower edge.

• Watch out for rear wheelarches. Any door skin which features a radius around a wheelarch will require a good deal of stretching in order to turn the return edge over and allow it to sit flat. This is achieved most quickly with your cross pien, though any uneven stretching will show as puckering on the door's front surface.

• Take care around swages. Soft feature lines can be lost due to poor positioning of the dolly, and a sharp strike with a cross pien is likely to stretch your skin.

• Door skinning tools are available, though I prefer not to use them.

• Sectional skin pieces are available for some models. These are often a false economy, however, and I would rather not use them.

• Corner and half round repairs can be made and fitted, however, in cases where the rot is very localised.

7-2a to 7-2c. Semicircular repair.

7-2a.

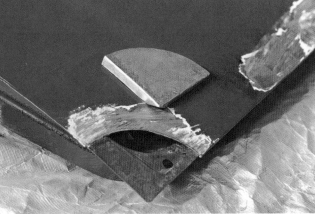

7-3. Corner repair section.

7-2b.

7-4. Aligning new door to old panels.

7-2c.

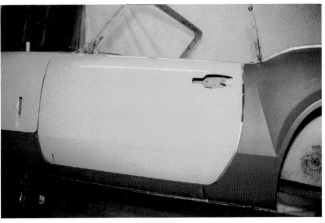

7-5. Aligning new panels to old door.

7-5a & 7-5b. Cutting frame joint.

7-6a to 7-6c. Repair to door bottom without removing skin.

7-6a.

7-5a.

7-6b.

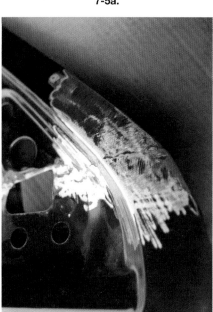

7-5b.

7-6c.

• In cases where the door skin extends around the window aperture, it's usual to cut-in the new panel, rather than fit the complete piece. In fact, many pattern skins will come pre-cropped. When deciding where exactly to make your cut, ease of access for welding, grinding and filling should be taken into consideration. Your painter may also have an opinion.
• Position your pre-cut skin in place over the old metal, and mark your provisional cut line with tape. Remove the old skin in the usual way, and cut to within half an inch (13mm) or so of the line. Remove the old skin, reposition the new metal, and scribe the exact final cut line onto

the door. Carefully make your final cut for the butt joint (some people prefer to hacksaw through the new and old metal simultaneously in order to ensure a perfect fit). Welding these joints is usually left until after the tapping up.

• Lower corner repair sections for the door frame can be made using card templates taken from the skin, or what was left of the frame, so as to achieve the correct angles. However, if you pre-cut this angle before shaping the piece, you'll often find that, in

7-7a & 7-7b. Fitting side impact bars during skinning.

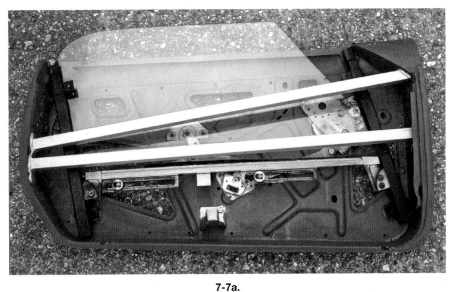

7-7a.

7-7b.

working the metal, it will have contracted across the corner. It's best, therefore, to work on a slightly oversized piece, and only cut the final angle when you've shaped it.

• A flexible body file can be employed to check and finish off the skin's face after tapping. Hold the file flat on the panel, parallel to the bottom edge, and pass it diagonally over the hammered area. This will both smooth any minor high points and reveal any lows.

• Zinc spray is a useful weapon against rust, a generous squirt on the mounting edge will reward you in the long run. Some etch primers will not adhere to zinc chromate, though, so check with your paint supplier or painter before coating anything on show.

• Seam sealer should be applied to the mounting edge inside the door. It should also be applied around the flange after tapping up, though this is often best left to your painter. You should seek advice from whomever will paint your door.

• For ease of handling, and a much reduced risk of hassle, you may opt to have your newly reskinned door painted on the car. This, obviously, requires that the inside of the door be sealed and painted first.

EXTRA SAFETY

Having spent many years involved with crash repair, and having lost a family member to a drunk-driver, safety is a very important issue for me. Some years ago I began offering custom-made, side-impact bars to my clients. They're not expensive and are easily fitted during door skinning. Get in touch via the publisher if you'd like more information on these.

Chapter 8
Sills, floors & outriggers

The heart of a good restoration, or a bad one for that matter, is the sill job. Regardless of whether your car has a separate chassis or is of unitary construction, the members that constitute the lower part of the door apertures are prone to rusting. If they're not dealt with properly, they will compromise the integrity of your vehicle's structure, and might leave you with ill fitting doors.

Sills vary hugely from vehicle to vehicle, so the exact method of replacement will have to be tailored to the model, as well as the degree of rot.

In its simplest form, the sill can be thought of as a box that runs between the A and B-posts. The sill members will communicate with the rest of the vehicle's structure via the A and B-posts and, in most cases, through outriggers that connect directly to the chassis rails. The other important piece to consider when looking at sills is the roof, which can be thought of as a compression member. If you have a soft top, then your sills have to work even harder in resisting the pressures to beam, bow or twist. A more detailed look at any sill will probably reveal

it to be made up of a collection of curves, steps and tapered facets. Typically, you'll have an inner and an outer section, and very often a blade or membrane sill running through the middle. It's not uncommon for part of the inner sill to be a continuation of the floor. The boxy nature of sills makes them ready water traps, and their proximity to the floor compounds this problem.

Replacing a sill, therefore, is not a job that can be considered in isolation. Removing a sill, or any part of it, requires that you brace the door aperture and support any connecting structures. The rust trap aspect often demands the replacement of floor and other sections at the same time.

The difficulty and expense of doing the job properly, coupled with low car values in the past, have led to many cars being bodged beyond belief in this area. I've seen too many cars with sills made of filler, foil and newspaper. One vehicle I recall had sills composed entirely of chicken wire and concrete. I've also seen an MGA sill/A-post combo made of fibreglass and timber!

TRIUMPH SPITFIRE SILLS & FLOOR
The Spitfire is a useful example here because it illustrates most of the problems you're likely to encounter. The Spitfire/GT6 family is a direct descendant of the earlier Herald and, it has to be said, the separate

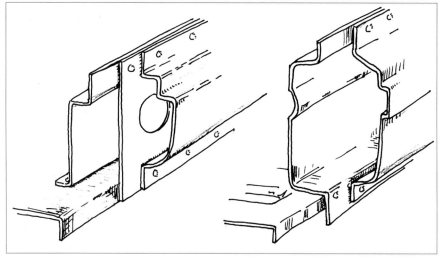

Typical sills.

Example 1.
8-1 to 8-18. Replace Spitfire sill and floor.

8-1. New panels laid out – a lot of metal!

8-4. ... outrigger and metal to go ...

8-2. Get the build straight in your mind with a trial assembly.

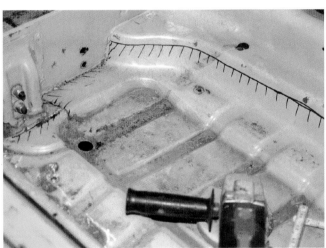

8-5. ... then cut line marked out. Make sure you check twice and cut once.

8-3. This had looked sound! Assess B-post ...

8-6. Floor comes out with great care ...

8-7. ... to leave a very big hole.

8-8. New floor goes in – beautiful welding.

8-9. Accurate location is critical ...

8-10. ... and closings made earlier.

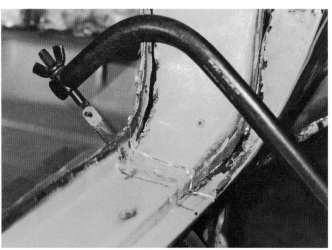

8-11. Hacksaw through sill after fixing floor in.

8-12. Unpick sill seam (OS) layer by layer ...

8-13. ... to reveal membrane is holed – YUCK!

8-14a & 8-14b. *Sans* sill.

8-14a. The car is well supported.

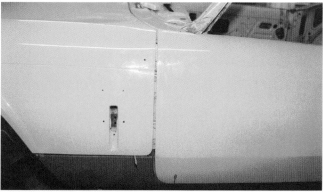

8-16. Mating inner sill to floor – spot welded before closing with outer panel.

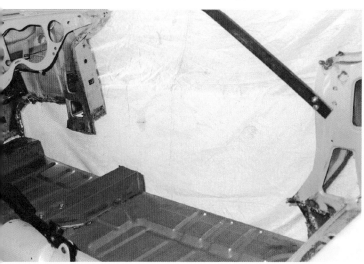

8-14b. Note brace across door gap.

8-17. Aligning outer sill to door and bonnet.

8-15. Poor repair found in OS rear has to be sorted out – now!

8-18. Car is ready for paint shop.

8-19. Alternative vehicle front assembly.

8-20. Previous repairs left unprotected.

chassis design was outdated even when it was new in the late 1950s.

The sills are basically made up of inner, membrane and outer sections. The floor runs under the inner piece, turns downwards, and mates with the membrane. The outer sill is spot welded along the bottom edge to both the membrane and the floor, and along the top to the membrane and inner sills. The design is such that if you follow the original build order, and work from the inside toward the outside, it's possible to use an electrical spot welder as access holes have been provided.

In order to properly fit the sills at the rear, some of the rear quarter panel may have to be sacrificed. The rear wing is not an expensive panel, though, and if the sills are rotten, this area will probably require some attention anyway.

Many of the Spitfires on the road today have very big door gaps at the front, but which fade to nothing at the lower rear corner. I've known of people trying to rectify this by grinding bits off the door! In fact, the problem is actually caused by the scuttle/A-post assembly creeping backward, and is a sure sign of sill trouble. Unfortunately, though, many of the cars displaying this malady have already had their sills replaced.

Another peculiarity of the Spitfire is that some of the points of attachment between the body and chassis are through the floor. This means that, in removing the floorpan, we will leave some of the body hanging in mid air, and prone to moving. If

you study the pictures, you'll see that the floor is 'boxy' at the front where it covers the outrigger, and also that the box section which crosses the floor and incorporates the seat mounting is effectively a continuation of the chassis. This piece sits on, and is bolted to, a diagonal facet of the chassis's truncated central outrigger.

Assessment

The first step in any job is to assess the condition of the metalwork, and so identify what appears to need to be replaced. I say appears because we don't have X-ray vision, of course, and these things tend to get worse as they are unpicked. So, grub around under the carpets, pick at any scabs, check the door gaps and scrape at the underseal.

As I said earlier, you can't deal with your sills in isolation, and the job shown here proves this point: as well as the sills, one entire floorpan needed replacement, as did both rear wings and much of the minor metalwork. Because I know the Spitfire is prone to flopping about like a jelly when the sills are removed, I opted to replace the floor before removing the sills, and to work on just one side at a time.

With any bodywork job, wading in and ripping out large amounts of rotten metal is a really bad idea. Although working around metal which you are later going to remove might seem like a waste of time, getting the job right is what counts in the end.

Familiarise yourself with the parts catalogue and don't remove anything until you have the new panels. It's also a good idea to assemble the new parts to each other with clamps, as this will reveal how well they are made, and will also give you a good idea about build order.

Along with your basic hand tools, you will need: a bumping hammer and flat dolly; an angle grinder with cutting, grinding, and flap discs; a heavy hammer and a sharp mortise chisel; a drill with 1/8 (3.5mm) bits and a spot weld drill; a hacksaw; as many mole grips and welding clamps as you can grab; a decent trolley jack; an assortment of wooden blocks; an old scissor jack or similar; and welding gear of some description (preferably MIG, and an electric spot welder). You'll also need all the relevant safety gear, of course, and some form of door aperture brace.

Set up & support

Because the Spitfire is reasonably rigid, due to its separate chassis, it's OK to set it on axle stands at a comfortable working height. The next step is to assess the door gaps (and make notes), then remove the door on the side you're working on. As you can see from the accompanying pictures, I've completely stripped out the interior.

This is because, when it comes to this sort of job, an empty car gives better access and removes any risk of fire damage to your trim. You probably won't need to go this far, though.

Once the time has come to remove the sill, the structure will need to be braced. Pairs of expandable door aperture braces are available, and I use them on larger cars, but I've found that they don't fit very well on the Spitfire. I have made my own braces from 5mm x 50mm mild steel plate, which I obtained from my local steel yard. This has been drilled at each end so that it can be bolted diagonally across the door gap, and allows the doors to be refitted. I also support the scuttle/bulkhead assembly with a scissor jack on top of the gearbox.

Work order

Decide on a work order (as best you can), and stick to it. In this case I've opted to make all the odds and sods required to make good the supporting structures first, as I fear that after the important panels have been removed, I may not have clear pointers with which to realign them.

The first major job is to remove the floor. Before this can be done, however, it's important to know that the new item will be correctly installed. With this in mind, I made up as many of the minor closing sections as possible, and clearly marked their position. In the case of the Spitfire floor, this usually means the rear outer corners where the floor joins the kick plate, and the front edge where it meets the bulkhead/firewall. Failure to address this problem early would have left me guessing as to the height of the floor, which, in turn, would have thrown off the line of the sill.

The next problem involved marking the position of the new floor before cutting out the old one. Due to the fact that the floor runs under the sill, it wasn't immediately possible to sit the new item exactly in place. In cases like this (... and there are many), you'll have to err on the side of safety. By measuring the floorpan and the depth of the new sill, it's possible to roughly mark the line where the new floor will sit, and then mark a cut line well in from it. Of course, you may not want to fit the complete floor, or you may find a positive location mark with which to align it. Watch out for hidden details under the floor, though, such as fuel lines and chassis rails.

Detach the floor where it mates with the sill. This is an obvious water trap and usually falls away with little resistance. The floor is spot welded along both its horizontal and vertical edges, where it meets the inner and membrane sill sections. Water from the road and inside the floorpan (... it's a soft top in England), along with any moisture within the sill itself, will have attacked this seam.

By running your chisel along the inside of the sill, the section of floor that mates with it can be severed. The waste material is then knocked off with the chisel, and the area cleaned up with a grinder. You can expect a few bits of sill to come off with the floor. The outrigger that spans the floor is also attached to the inner sill. If you wish to retain or replace the outrigger, then it must be carefully unpicked at the sill end. This member is unusual in that it sits inside the car, whereas most outriggers run underneath the floor. To separate the member from the floorpan cleanly, you'll have to drill out the welds from underneath. This can be performed after the floor has been removed, though.

Split around the front and rear seams in a similar manner, leaving the waste edge to be unpicked later.

The inboard cut can be made with a grinder (you could use the chisel, of course, though this would necessitate more tidying up). The exact location of the cut line through the floor needs to be considered carefully. It's often difficult to tidy up after welding, and we don't want to create another water trap, or leave a scar that will upset the MoT tester. I usually join the floor from above with a continuous string of overlapping MIG welds on the inside, and punctuated stitches underneath. While this is perfectly strong enough, it's not always obvious from the underside of the car what has been done. If you have access to a resistance spot welder, then spot welds spaced 1/2in apart should produce an original looking seam. Whichever method of welding you employ, the overlap should not be more than about 20mm.

With the old floor out and the adjacent panels tidied up, trial fit the new floor and mark a final cut line. The floor can then be removed, and the final cut made. The area around the final weld line is cleaned up and given a coat of zinc spray, before the floor is positioned for fixing. In order to allow the new floor to sit correctly, support it with a jack and a length of timber under the sill edge. Although working to a sill that is later to be replaced is not the quickest way of working, and you may be tempted to not clean it up properly, be warned that anything that throws the floor offline could seriously hinder your efforts later. With this in mind, it's a matter for your judgement as to when best to fix the closing pieces to the peripheral structures. Having the inner sill in place makes lining up the new outrigger very easy, though welding it in is best left until the old sill assembly is out.

When the new floor is in place,

you can now line up the new outrigger before removing the sill. As the complete assembly is to be replaced, the centre section can be removed with a hacksaw. The ends and any points which connect with adjacent panels will then have to be drilled and unpicked.

On the Spitfire, the rear of the outer sill stops just under the rear wing, while the membrane is attached to (and might be considered a continuation of) the inner rear quarter panel. The inner sill extends beyond the membrane, and attaches to the same panel on its inside (see accompanying pictures 8-12, 8-13 and 8-16). The lower part of the rear quarter panel, therefore, has to be removed in order to replace the outer sill. In this case, though, the complete rear wing was due for renewal, so I left most of this panel in place for the time being. Removing the complete rear quarter panel would have allowed undue movement, and would have left me without a shut line to work to when I trial fitted the door.

At the front of the assembly, the outer sill sweeps up to run parallel to the bonnet's lower edge, and takes in the front lower corner of the door shut line. The sill's fore and aft location are critical, therefore, to the door's fit, and to the position of the bonnet. Any deviation in placement of the A-post/scuttle assembly caused by it having fallen backward, will make correct alignment of the sills impossible.

The membrane sill connects with the lower section of the A-post, which mirrors the front of the outer sill in the way that it forms an expanded section of sill. The inner sill also closes to the lower A-post section. The front opening of the sill is closed by a small plate, and can be left until last without worry.

The lower section of our A-post only required a small repair where the firewall sits upon it (this particular bit of rust wasn't apparent until the outer sill was removed). I prefer to drill out as many of the visible welds as possible, before splitting around with the chisel. This then leaves me with the drilled waste edges to unpick using the chisel and mole grips. Wherever possible, I mark on the new floor any relevant information that will help with the rebuild, such as the position of the rear of the inner sill (see pics 8-9, 8-10).

Having removed all the gash metal from the sill, and tidied up the supporting structures, I set the new sill pieces in place prior to welding them in. The keys to rebuilding the Spitfire are the build order and the location of the A-post (as I said earlier, the build order is basically a case of working from the floor outwards). The problem, however, is that in order to check that everything lines up correctly, the door needs to be hung and the gap checked.

This, of course, means that the sill assembly has to be aligned and fitted, but not fixed permanently until we're certain that it is 100 per cent right.

As the new floor was set to the old sill, I could trust it to give me the height of the inner sill. The fore and aft position is set by the marks I put on the floor earlier, while the lateral location is governed by the floor edge, the outrigger, and the panels at each end to which the inner sill joins.

The membrane sill closes the box formed by the inner sill and is very difficult to misalign, other than to misjudge the angle at which the front mates to its counterpart. Obviously, the inner sill must be fixed along its bottom edge to the floor, before the membrane is fitted. Since we're only talking about a trial fitting, the outer panels will need to be removed again later. The ends of the membrane sill can be accessed through the holes in the inner sill.

The location of the outer sill is governed by the line of the inner and membrane sill pieces, and the front top edge of the panel runs over the seam where the inner A-post meets the A-post proper and aligns with the bonnet's lower edge. As you can see from my pictures, I didn't have the bonnet attached when I started the job, but you must have it attached so you're not left guessing!

With the sill assembly pop riveted in place, I fitted the door to ensure the correct alignment of the A-post and scuttle. Even with the brace in situ, it is possible to lift the A-post just enough to alter the door gap.

If your car refuses to line up, make a diagram of the door and its adjacent panels with the gap errors exaggerated. This will highlight where the fault lies, and you'll soon sort out the problem. As the A-post/scuttle assembly is known to move, and the sill is not original, the only line I know to be true is the rear of the door gap. By setting the door hinges to the middle of their travel and then closing the door, I get a good idea of where the A-post is in relation to where it should be. I can then correct it by looking at the gaps along the new sill and the B-post. The acid test, however, is when the bonnet is closed. If things are where they should be, the front door gap and the gap between the bonnet and scuttle line should be even and similar in width to the other gaps. The top of the wing should align to the top of the door, and the bottom of the wing should align with the top front of the sill. A minor tweak to the bonnet's height at the front is often required to get this line perfect.

When you're entirely happy with the gaps, remove the door for the last time, and remove the outer and membrane sill panels. The inner sill is then spot welded to

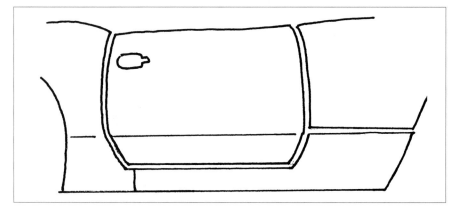

Example of door fit diagram. You can cut out the panels and exaggerate the gap faults. This will highlight the problems.

and/or weight, and even a sound example of this model when lifted unevenly will appear distressed if the doors are opened!

The sill sections are pretty impressive pieces of work. The inner sill is of a very heavy gauge, by the standards of the day, and spans the full length between the wheelarches. The rear chassis and suspension are fixed to a crossmember which mates to, and is dependant on, the the rear of the inner sill. The inner rear quarter panel and B-post also sit on the inner sill. At the front, the inner sill butts up to the inner arch and supports the firewall. Two outriggers run laterally under the floor, between the inner sill and the front chassis members. Furthermore, the chassis rails don't run the full length of the car, and so rely on the sill assembly to take the load.

Example 2. 8- 21 to 8-28. Removing Stag outer sill.

8-21. Shot-blasted shell arrives.

8-22. Revealing filler and rot ...

the floor, and MIG welded at the front and rear. The membrane is then replaced and aligned to the hole left by the rivets which had previously held it. The membrane should only need a few welds to hold it along its length for now. As I pointed out earlier, the front and rear of the membrane are accessed for spot welding through holes in the inner sill.

The next step is to reposition the outer sill and fix it with spot welds (through the inner and membrane along the top edge, and through the membrane and floor along the bottom). The rear of the outer sill sits over the foot of the B-post and has to be spot MIG'ed, while the front top edge is mated to the outside of the firewall/A-post assembly. The foot of the A-post is a separate closing, and can be fixed to the sill before fitment or, as in this case, fitted after the sill by means of a combination of MIG and electrical spot welds.

As all of the alignment problems are due to questions about the front edge, it's possible to fix the sill in place along its length and at the rear, but leave the front free to move. After the appropriate tweaking, then, the front could be welded in.

The job is completed when the rear quarter panel (or part of it) is replaced, as the sill sits under this panel for about 1/2in.

THE TRIUMPH STAG

The Stag is a very different beast to the Spitfire, despite the family relationship. The Stag doesn't have a separate chassis, for example, and the sills are really quite massive. Also, the Stag is very prone to 'beaming' (flexing) along its length, so the only safe way to tackle the sills is with the car sat on its wheels. Early press releases show that the design was originally intended to have double inner and outer sills, which would have greatly added to its rigidity. However, the car was finally launched with a simple two-part sill assembly, presumably to keep down costs

8-23. ... and more rot.

8-26. ... a nice surprise – internals, not bad ...

8-24. Ed opens window in RQP ...

8-27. ... unlike post feet which show rot.

8-25. ... to reveal ...

8-28. Original red oxide is a good sign. Note expanding brace.

The outer sill panel is the same length as the inner, and nearly as heavy. It has a pronounced taper, thinning toward the rear, and the flat on its topside continues beyond the span of the door aperture. Behind the door, the rear quarter panel sits atop the sill, as does the foot of the B-post. Forward of the door, the A-post also sits on the outer sill, while the front wing wraps around it, and is fixed along the lower edge. Therefore, to replace the outer sill, it's necessary to remove part of the front wing and open a window in the rear quarter panel. In practice, however, the section of the rear quarter panel that sits above the sill is a water trap, and always requires replacement at the same time.

The story at the front, however, is not so fortuitous as it's not uncommon to find cars whose sills have been replaced without the removal of the front wings. In many of these cases, the sills have simply been chopped and tucked with no regard to structural integrity. In other cases, upon removing a wing for replacement, for example, the sills have been found to be rotten because the lower part of the wing tends to hold water and dirt against the outer face of the sill.

The sill assembly is closed by the front inner wheelarch, and this area is another known water trap. Both the A and B-post feet are prone to rotting where they run onto the outer sill.

The only vestiges of the original double outer sill are the two jacking points, which consist of straps of metal between the top and bottom edges, and a stud which is screwed into a captive nut, through a hole in the bottom. Many owners opt to ignore these jacking points, however, as they're not really suitable for supporting the car!

So, with the car sitting on its wheels, and stripped of trim as required, begin by cutting a window from the rear quarter panel to gain access to the rear of the sill. The depth of this window will be governed by the amount of access required. Having dealt with many of these cars, I am happy to 'chop-in' the outer sill around the inner rear quarter panel mounting in order to avoid a lot of unnecessary work, but only in cases where this area of the original is sound. Likewise, the front of the outer sill is accessed by removing all or part of the lower wing and, in a few cases, it's acceptable to chop in the new outer sill around the base of the A-post. The shape of the sill allows for very accurate location and very strong welding, but failure to chop the sill in correctly might compromise the integrity of the vehicle's structure. So, when in doubt ... don't!

Before removing any of the sill, insert a brace across the door aperture. I use one of the expanding variety for the Stag, though, of course, you may prefer to make your own. You can't be too careful when it comes to bracing the Stag. In fact, I tend to double up on the repair side and, on one

particularly rotten car I remember, I even braced the side that I hadn't yet started!

Because the bottoms of the A and B-posts tend to rust (and are no longer available), I usually fabricate my own repair sections for these areas before hacking into the metalwork too much. Furthermore, if I'm going to chop-in the sill, then I'll take advantage of these repairs to cover the part of my join which might otherwise be visible.

Begin the process of removing the outer sill by drilling the visible spot welds which run the full length of the top and bottom. I tend to leave the top welds fore and aft of the door shut in place to begin with, as a question mark hangs over whether I'll use the complete sill. Next, using a cutting disk on the grinder, cut around the disputed areas (see pic 8-27). The other detail that needs to be addressed is the remains of the jacking point, which is (or was) attached to the top of the inner sill by a strap, and, if not separated, will hold the sill panel in place. The bottom of the strap is fixed by four spot welds which can be drilled or cut around. It's often the case with cars of this age, that the line of welds along the bottom does not require drilling. You'll probably find that water sitting in the seam has thinned the metal so much that it's weakened to a point where it will let go without much of a fight. When this happens you're left with the remnants of the weld and flange which can be cleaned off with your grinder. The welds which have been drilled will probably need a little persuasion from your chisel before they will allow the sill to fall away to reveal the state of the inner sill section.

The inner sill is prone to rusting at its

front, where it's met by the front outrigger, and at the rear, where the member which carries the suspension joins the sill. In both of these instances, the rust is due to water in the adjoining member rather than in the sill itself (initially, at least).

It's fairly rare for the inner sill to require complete replacement, more commonly a local repair section will suffice, which is just as well as it's a big job, and the replacement panels which are available do not fit so well. Any repairs to the inner sill must, of course, be carried out properly, using material of the correct gauge, and mustn't interfere with the alignment of the outer panel.

New outer sills are pressed using the original dies and are of very high quality. Before fitting the outer sill, clean off the black primer that it is supplied in and apply a coat of zinc to the faces that close against the inner sill. Positioning the new sill is fairly straightforward; the height is set by the inner sill and the fore and aft positions are governed by the closings at either end. Expect a minor tweak to get it perfect (normally a case of clamping the sill in place and tapping with a club hammer until perfection is achieved). When you're happy with the sill's alignment, a few 3.5mm pop rivets or PKs can be employed as temporary fixings.

To confirm the correct position of the sill, you'll need to re-hang the door, though, in most cases, simply sitting the door onto its hinges and closing it will suffice. The catch at the rear of the door will hold it on line and, if need be, a wedge of card under the front can be used to lift it. If the front wing has been removed, the new one will also have to be trial fitted at this point.

With the wing and door in situ, check the line of the sill (it should be even), and when it looks good strip away the wing and door again and set-to with the welder. If it's not even, re-tweek and try again. Although this can be pretty tiresome, it's the only way to guarantee getting the job right. The holes left by the rivets can be used as datum points for adjustment, and will need to be MIG welded later.

The seam along the door shut is best spot welded but, as the panels tend to pull away from each other, and are of a heavy gauge, clamp the pieces tightly prior to welding. The seam along the bottom can be spot welded for most of its length, but access is restricted toward the rear and behind the outriggers. I drill and 'spot MIG' these areas. The inside of the seam has to be stripped of underseal and paint prior to the welding, which can be pretty tedious, so it's tempting to simply 'plug MIG' the lot, and grind it all off later (should one give in to such temptation).

The A-post and forward section are

8-29. Removing complete sill at front.

best MIG welded. If you've removed the whole sill, then this means welding through the holes left by drilling out the original welds. If you've opted to chop-in the sill, then you now have to join the new panel to the remains of the old. Any overlap in the join must be dressed so as to allow the new sill and any adjoining pieces to sit flush.

The area aft of the door is also best fixed with MIG, and is more often chopped-in, since to remove all of the original is rather fiddly and usually unnecessary. The step in the sill allows for perfect alignment, especially when the hole at the rear is used as a fore/aft datum. Again, the quality of welding is critical.

Any excess weld around the area of the post feet will need to be cleaned off before the repair sections are installed. Both the A and B-posts taper downward and sit upon the sill. The original spot welds appear to have been formed before the outer and inner sills were mated and cannot be replicated, so the MIG welder is the only option. When fixing in these sections, a little care must be taken to ensure that any excess weld can be removed with the grinder without causing damage. A mini belt sander is very handy for details like this.

To finish the job, the rear quarter panel must be made good (or replaced), and the same is true of the front wing (which needs its bottom replacing). The lowest edge of the wing is welded through the sill and, as it's also on line with the front outrigger, this is a job for the MIG. Any proud weld left from the sill welding operation will throw the wing out of line. (See picture 6/8a in chapter 6.)

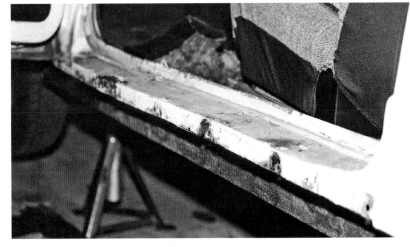

8-31. Tread-plate as was.

8-32. Removal with chisel after drilling ...

8-30. New sill cut-in at rear.

Tread-plate sills on a separate chassis car

When Tony Beadle first brought his little Herald to me, with a view to sorting out the tread-plates and bolting on a new pair of sills, I looked the job over but didn't bother to lift the carpets. Instead, I assumed the

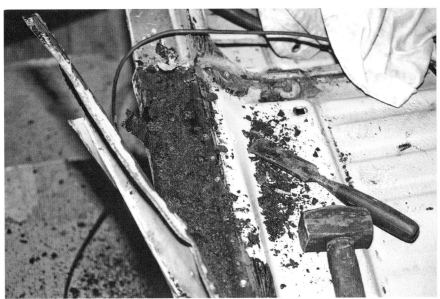

8-33. The ugly truth looks pretty sad.

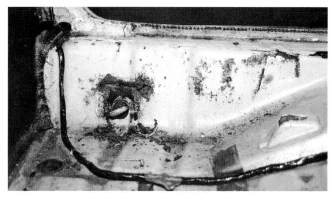

8-34. Floor and seatbelt anchor.

8-35. Rot removed. It's not safe – ready for new.

8-36. New metal needs tidying.

8-37. New inner section – "I made that!"

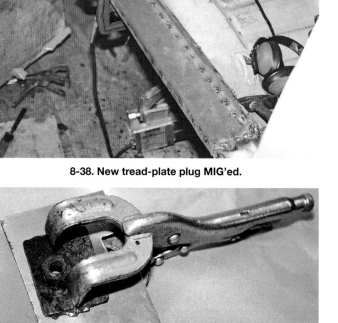

8-38. New tread-plate plug MIG'ed.

8-39. Seatbelt anchor rebuilt – safety is critical.

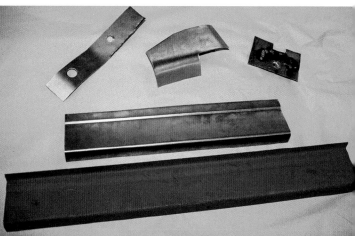

8-40. All the new metal. Most had to be made.

floors to be sound where they met the door shuts. Lesson one: assume nothing!

The Herald is actually an ideal candidate for this process, and is about the only Triumph that doesn't require a brace across the door aperture.

As with any job, the first thing to do is to decide how much needs doing. Obviously, some knowledge of the car's structure will help, as will a clear field of view (so when it comes to stripping out, you can never go too far). The interiors of these cars are simple, but expect every nut to be seized (a liberal squirt of WD40 beforehand will pay dividends).

The Herald has a seam running across the floor where the front and rear floorpans overlap and are bolted through to the chassis. There is (or was), a strap of webbing between the two sheets of metal and this is an obvious water trap. The rear floorpan extends under the tread-plates, and it's where the two layers run common that the tin-worms feast. The top tread-plate is spot welded though to the floor along the outer edge, where the outer sill is screwed on, and along the top just out from the door rubber flange. This piece also extends an inch or so under the foot of the B-post and is welded through. If the post foot is sound, it's quite legitimate to lop the new tread-plate short and butt-weld it in.

Reveal the position of the spot welds with a bit of emery and drill them out with a cobalt drill. Aim to cut through only the top layer, though.

The condition of the metal under the tread-plate is not always clear, even with a look underneath, so your best bet is to unpick the top metal carefully, but be prepared for the worst. As you can see i the accompanying pictures, the driver's side appeared to have been dealt with, though the welding was clearly not brilliant. Removal of the new top piece, however, revealed the underlying metal to be completely rotten. Repair section are easily fabricated and need not be perfect. The size of your repair pieces will, of course, be governed by the extent of the rot. I found the best way to work was to make sections for the tread area and floor/inner-sill area separately, and then overlap them when required. Use card or paper to make templates, and make up the new pieces before chopping out the rot. This is where the question of where to stop becomes important. I was originally asked to deal with the sills, but, of course, if the metal that the sill attaches to is rotten ... Likewise, a dodgy seatbelt mount cannot be ignored. An angle grinder with a cutting disc will make short work of removing the rotten metal, but be certain to cover any trim, etc, which might be damaged by the sparks. Grinder blast is hot enough to pit glass and ignight poly-cotton overalls, so beware.

Having made the new metal, draw around it and allow for any overlap you think appropriate. I opted for butt welding, except for the piece with the seatbelt anchor (for reasons of strength this had a 1/2in overlap).

Before closing up, treat all internal metal with a rust neutraliser and a coat of zinc spray (it may be expensive, but it's good stuff).

New outer sills come without any screw holes, for some reason, but the easiest way to mark them up for drilling is to use the original sill from the opposite side, turned upside down and laid along the top of the new piece. You will note that the holes are elongated, so it's not as simple a job as it might be.

HALF SILL SECTION
& OVERSILLS
Half sill

Given the structural nature of the sill member, it is questionable as to whether a half sill section is appropriate. That said, if you do opt for this method of repair, you had better know how to get it right.

I have only fitted half sill sections during crash repairs, though I do often chop-in sills around post feet and in some respects this amounts to much the same thing.

The first thing to do, of course, is to decide exactly how much of the new sill you are going to put in, and where you're going to join it. Should you also opt to perform the same trick with the inner sill, then it's imperative that the two panels have their respective joints at least 150mm (preferably more) apart, to avoid setting up a weak point along the sill's length. See the accompanying diagram for the correct method of forming the joint.

The oversill

An oversill is a sill panel which has been pressed slightly oversized so as to allow it to be welded over the original as a quick fix.

I can't say that I am a fan of the oversill but, in some instances, such panels are all that is available. The Triumph saloon in the accompanying picture is a case in point, and the panel as supplied by the owner is not a great pressing and does not span the full length of the original. The front of the new sill is designed to be tucked under the front wing and forgotten. This is not acceptable, however, and appropriate repair sections will have to be fabricated to make good any deficiencies. The other problem with this type of panel is that because the new piece is to be sat over the old, your door gap is in danger

8-41a to 8-41e. Use of oversill.

8-41a.

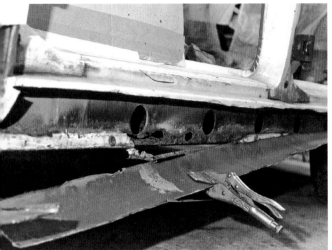

8-41b.

8-41d.

8-41c.

8-41e.

of being lost. In this particular case, the new sills do not allow for the door shut at all, so I opted to tuck the top edge behind the originals for the full length, in a manner which will allow a skim of filler to hide the join. Had the sill treads proved rusty, then I would have made up new sections as required. In truth, had the new sill covered the tread, I probably would have chopped them and carried out the job in exactly the same way as I am now! Interestingly, the new panels reach beneath the car, beyond the limit of the original sill, and take in a section which is an extension of the membrane sill. Whoever decided on this was not concerned with originality, but obviously new where these cars rusted.

Chapter 9
Chassis members – repair & renewal

As far as the majority of European and Japanese motor manufacturers are concerned, the separate chassis was out-moded decades ago, though vestiges of it have lingered. Many of the cars we know and love are direct descendants of models which predate the monocoque, while many more illustrate the designers' lack of experience with chassis-less structures.

9-1. This rather sad Mazda clearly shows the concept of the modern 'chassis.'

Lotus-type backbone chassis.

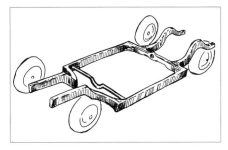

USA-style peripheral chassis.

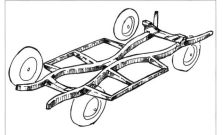

British 60s sports car chassis.

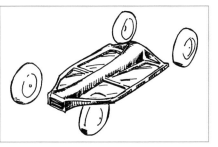

VW floorpan chassis.

For example, a critical look at the underpinnings of the MG A and B models will reveal a few familial links, despite these two cars having very different design philosophies.

OK, so before anyone starts knocking holes in their vehicle's most critical supports, it might be a good idea to get an understanding of what a chassis is and what it does.

The earliest metal chassis designs date back to the horse and cart, and consisted of a simple ladder of iron rails and braces from which the cart springs and front steering pivot would have been hung. The members would originally have been joined with rivets. As steels improved, and a greater understanding of the vehicle's specific needs grew, so the basic ladder was lightened and adapted to flow around the axles. Welding of the frame and a myriad of other detail changes later, and we arrive at the sort of structure we now know.

The strength and integrity of the chassis are essential if the vehicle is to behave in the correct manner in any given situation. Therefore, before any repair is carried out, it's imperative that the chassis be in correct alignment. **Caution!** Before I go any further, I must state categorically that if you suspect your chassis to be deficient or out of alignment, then you must hand it over to an experienced professional for correction. Your life may depend upon your car doing what you expect it to. As small time restorers, therefore, we are limited in terms of what we can do to our chassis, to replacing outriggers, crossmembers, and patching up holes in the main rails.

THE BASIC CHECKS
Lift check
The simplest test of integrity, for most European sports cars with a separate chassis, is to remove one rear lamp and lift the car from the lamp hole. If the rear of the door gap closes as the car is raised, then you obviously have a problem (though this might simply mean your sills need attention).

Drop check
This is the traditional method of checking a car's alignment, and is a fairly low-tech but valid technique.

Set the car on a clean and level floor and, working from the back forwards, drop a plum bob from as many symmetrical points on your chassis as you can find, and mark the point where the bob touches the floor. When you have marked as many points as is practical from the entire length of the vehicle, join them up by marking diagonal lines between pairs of front and rear marks. If your car is true, then the pairs of diagonal lines should all converge along one centre line.

A little deductive reasoning will tell you where any deviation lies, and any rise in the chassis should reveal itself as foreshortening.

The jig
The alignment jig comes in many forms these days. In its simplest form, the jig is a steel bed, onto which customised brackets are bolted. These brackets align with, and often bolt to, specific points on the vehicle's body or suspension. Assuming frontal damage is suspected, it's normal practice to start mounting the jig brackets from the rear of the vehicle until a misregister is found. The weight of the body is not borne by the jig brackets, but by substantial clamps, against which any pulling can be performed. As the damage is rectified, so the bracketing process can be completed. Replacement panels can also be aligned and fixed using the brackets for support.

Bracket-less jigs usually consist of a giant measuring gauge, which sits under the car, upon which several telescopic pointers are mounted and aligned to given points on the vehicle. The data needed to carry out the test for each vehicle is supplied by the jig manufacturer.

Newer jig systems often incorporate measurements of higher structures, such as door gaps and pillars. Some use laser alignment, in which case targets are dropped from strategic points and a beam passed through them. Most alignment systems give an option for suspension 'in' or 'out' measurement.

While jig systems can be hired, their use by the amateur restorer is not recommended.

OUTRIGGERS
Regardless of whether your car has a separate chassis or is of unitary construction, the outriggers can prove problematic. The first of the following examples typifies the job of renewing a pair of outriggers on a separate chassis vehicle, while the second (my old favourite, the Stag), illustrates what you might find on the average unitary body.

Example 1
If you own a Triumph Herald or Vitesse, then you'll almost certainly need a pair of rear outriggers. These components are especially prone to rot, and problems here will get spotted at MoT time.

Given that rotten outriggers are an MoT failure, and also that they help locate the rear axle, the quality of your welding is going to be critical. So, if you can handle a MIG welder and you're not claustrophobic, read on.

Replacing the outrigger is actually a pretty straightforward job. In fact, with a bit of planning, both outriggers can be replaced in a single day. What held me up last time I did this job was the fuel lines (I tried to move one and found it to be a bit fragile – petrol leaks and welding do not mix). Consider this before you commit yourself to the project, and pre-soak any nuts and bolts in advance with WD40 or penetrating oil to make the job that bit easier.

Along with the usual hand tools and safety gear, you'll need at least one pair of decent axle stands, a good jack, a good angle grinder with cutting discs, and a sharp mortise chisel (asbestos hands would also be useful). Keep a fire extinguisher to hand, and a pot of Cold Front ceramic paste is handy for protecting the fuel lines.

The first step is to set the car squarely on the axle stands and remove the rear road wheels. Next, take a wire brush to the nuts and bolts that hold the swing arm brackets and body tub. Give everything a good soaking with WD40, but be prepared to lose a couple of nuts and bolts (if they give too much grief, cut them

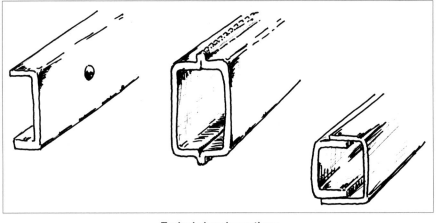

Typical chassis sections.

9-2 to 9-8. Replacing outriggers on separate chassis vehicle.

9-2. Unsafe (an MoT failure in the UK) – note fuel lines.

9-3. The offending article now shows its true condition.

9-4. New members are sided (handed). Don't swap them!

9-5. Ready to weld. Zinc spray protects and conducts.

9-6. Inboard welding – safety critical.

9-7. Outboard joint and repair located by bolt to corner of body tub ...

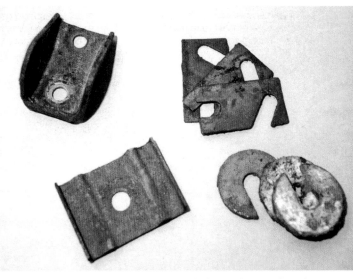

9-8. ... and the rest. Any rusty nuts and bolts are best replaced.

off with a grinder or hacksaw and replace later with new, high-tensile, or preferably stainless, items).

Next, clean around the ends of the outriggers, removing all mud, rust and underseal (the chisel is useful here), and make a location mark with a hacksaw blade on the chassis, so that you can exactly replace the member. The bolt from the body tub is your datum for the outside. If you can't leave a positive location mark at each end, you might consider dropping a plum line from the bracket holes and marking on the floor. This technique may have been used by Noah, but it still works.

Note! if you are working with the fuel lines in place, make a guard from a piece of 20swg (1in x 1in x 6in), and tuck this behind them.

The final step is simply to chop off the rotten outrigger with your cutting disc and chisel. I've found that these pieces don't resist too much (in fact, you have to watch out for the outside end falling away with too much of the sidemember).

Grind off any remnants of outrigger from the chassis and make good the sidemember ready to receive the new box sections. A good squirt of zinc spray will help conduct the new weld and provide some rust protection.

The new outriggers come covered in red oxide primer, and require no special preparations other than to scrape the paint off the joint areas before welding. Position the new part using your saw cut and the bolt from the bodywork (plus spacers), and, when you're happy with the fit, weld it into the chassis.

The MoT test specifies continuous welding and a car can fail on any breaks

or 'snotty-looking' bits in the weld. If any part is deficient, grind it off and overweld it. That said, it's a good job the MoT tester can't see above the chassis really, because we can't reach there!

Cover everything in another coat of zinc, not forgetting the bracket area, and apply a coat of Hammerite, or similar, over the job before bolting it all back together again (having first cleaned and coated the spacers, etc).

Needless to say, the job would have been a lot easier and more thorough with the body off the chassis.

A bit more on safety & fuel lines
From the point of view of the home restorer, having the fuel lines pass though the chassis outriggers was never a great idea. As I said earlier, although these lines can appear sound, they will fracture very easily if disturbed. If you detect any petrol fumes, or if you're in any doubt, don't weld (petrol must always be treated with respect). For the job, I opted to replace the lines with rubber hose after draining the tank. Other options include using a tubular sleeve to protect the fuel lines, or packing them in 'Cold Front' ceramic paste and wrapping them in foil. Whatever you do, don't allow the lines to get hot or to earth the welder!

Example 2
The problems associated with the outriggers on the Triumph Stag are pretty typical of the sort you'll encounter. Firstly, thes inverted top-hat sections are closed by the floor, and so often fill up with rust. Secondly, in many cases the outer few inches

which mate to the sill decay at a much faster rate than the rest of the member, so a local repair is not out of the question. Finally, the available replacements are not exactly true to the originals, so making your own is an option. See accompanying diagram. Also see picture 9-11.

To completely remove an outrigger, start by drilling out the welds from inside the car (when the time comes, you can use the same holes to weld through), then separate the outrigger from the chassis and sill. From experience, I doubt the sill end will fight back.

After cleaning up any gash metal, set the new outrigger in place with the aid of a jack, and begin welding from the chassis end before adding a few tacks to hold the sill end. With the jack applying a slight lifting pressure, the new member should sit tight against the floor. If it does not, then drill 1/8in (3.5mm) holes and use a few well-placed PKs to pull everything together.

REPAIRS TO CHASSIS MAIN RAILS
Repairs to the chassis's main members or crossmembers are governed by the same guidelines as the replacement of outriggers and sills, though when dealing with the main rails you may have to work with large sections of heavy gauge metal (heavy by motor vehicle standards anyway). Also, it's not unusual to find reinforcements either outside or hidden inside. In some cases, it is the double layer which acts as the water trap which, in turn, causes the corrosion. One particular model with which I am well

9-9a. This MGB appeared sound ...   **9-9b&c. ... but a closer look revealed the truth.**

9-10. Typical chassis rot, at lowest point.

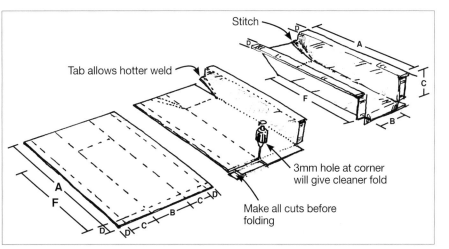

Stitch

Tab allows hotter weld

3mm hole at corner will give cleaner fold

Make all cuts before folding

Typical outrigger. Tailor details as required.

9-11. Integral chassis closed by floorpan.

9-12. Mini sills span between sub-frames. Wheels are for ballast.

versed shows this very clearly. The front legs run down to meet the bulkhead so that the rails which emerge from under the car overlap the leg section. Being as this is the lowest point, any moisture in the leg will run down and sit between the two layers of metal. The result is that what should be one of the strongest points on the car, is potentially one of the weakest!

Any attempt to repair or renew substantial elements of the chassis must involve a lot of support and very strong welding. Again, when in doubt ... don't! Leave it to the experts.

Another hidden danger lurking in the chassis box sections is wax injection. I've had experience of wax flaring up explosively during the repair process, and believe me, it's not a lot of laughs.

Miscellaneous

The nature of chassis repair is such that you may well have to deal with some miscellaneous rot. Some knowledge of your car's structure will help greatly at these times. Here is a selection of the sort of things I am talking about, along with how I have dealt with them.

9-13a to 9-13c. It gets worse before it gets better.

9-13a.

9-13b.

9-13c.

9-14. Internal box member.

9-15a & 9-15b. Dog-leg repair.

9-15a.

9-15b.

• Dog-leg repair. The dog-leg at the base of the windscreen of many sports cars is bit of a water trap, and it's rare to find decent repair sections for any model. In cases of minor corrosion, the rust can simply be displaced by MIG weld and then faced off. For more advanced rot, the new piece has to be made. Clever use of a paper template and a bit of dressing on the car (of the new section), are usually the order of the day. Beware the hidden detail, and remember that there's little point in making good the exterior panel if the inner piece is rotten.
This may also be a safety issue.

• The inner sill repair. One extreme example of an inner sill repair was this car, on which the inner sill had all but let go of the crossmember. The subframe hung from the crossmember which, in turn held the semi-trailing arms. From experience I knew the replacement inner sills to be very poor in this area, so I opted to fabricate my own repair sections.

• The crossmember repair. Continuing on from the previous example, the rear crossmember also proved to be deficient, and not available. Had the owner not spent so much money on this vehicle to date I might have advised scrapping it. To make the sections of the crossmember, I had to first make up a hammer form which was used to shape the recesses which located the bushes and bolts.

• The rear chassis section replacement. With any soft top, there is always danger of water ingress. This vehicle was not in bad shape, but what looked at a glance to be a bit of localised scabbing around the rear spring seats turned out to be major rot damage. There was no alternative but to replace both chassis legs between the main crossmember which supports the rear suspension and the minor rear crossmember that spans the end of the chassis.

The main concern involves properly supporting the car, so I set it on every axle stand and wooden block that I could get my hands on. After this, the job was a simple matter of drilling the old legs out from above, and cutting through the rails with an air saw and a cutting disk on my grinder.

9-16a & 9-16b. Inner sill repair.

9-17a & 9-17b. Inner sill, chassis leg, and crossmember repair sections.

9-16a.

9-17a.

9-17b.

9-16b.

Boot floor

Typical rear spring-hanger.

9-18. This car has just received new rear chassis legs.

I held the new pieces in place with a jack and tacked from the sides, before stud welding through the floor, and finished off with some hot MIG welding after the jack was removed. The new spring seats are supplied separately and were added afterward.

Chapter 10
More about floors

If you wanted to provoke a piece of steel sheet into corroding then, short of using it to toboggan down Brighton beach, you could not find a better method than using it as a car's floor. Road spray, wet feet, and any moisture that finds its way into the vehicle, will collect around the floor and attack it from every angle. Many of the early attempts at protection, such as underseals and bituminous pads,

have only exacerbated the corrosion by separating from the panel's surface and retaining water, which has then done further damage.

The Spitfire floor featured in the previous section was available in either whole of half form. The complete item makes for a neater job, of course, but the half floor would have been far easier to handle (incidentally, I often prefer half

sections). Furthermore, many of the available replacement floors are not very good pressings, and very few are true to the original.

The floorpan is more than just a flat piece of steel. It has many flutes and indentations formed into it which are primarily to stop the panel from 'drumming,' though in some cases these channel water towards a drain plug. Other

10-1. Not a sink drainer.

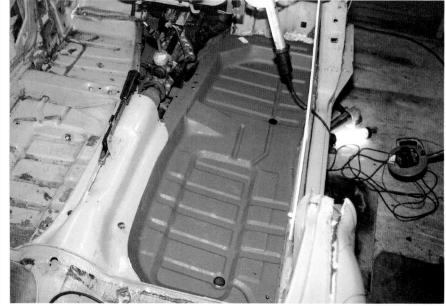

10-2. Large piece nicely pressed – but tricky to handle.

10-3. New floor sections each side with old and new box chassis mounting sections.

10-4. Removing old floor, working around previous repairs, and sub-structures.

10-5. The bulk is out.

10-6. Separate seat runner from floor.

10-7. Old seat runner, new floor.

shaping is usually a means of gaining legroom. You may also notice four large holes which have been covered by circular plates. These were used as part of the location system during manufacture and can be ignored.

You should also expect to find seat and seatbelt anchorage points attached to your floor, and these can be anything from a nut welded underneath to a set of box sections. These additions to the floor need careful consideration, since incorrect replacement could have serious consequences in a collision. It's also not uncommon to find the seat mounting rails bridging between the floor and sill.

You can expect to find at least one outrigger under your floor and, in many cases the floor will run into the sill, and may even constitute a part of it.

Generally speaking, removing a floor or part of it will not compromise the structure of the car. Although the floor does add something to the overall rigidity of the vehicle, its primary function is to stop you from falling onto the road. The section of floor which sits between the chassis rails and takes in the transmission tunnel, is usually protected from corrosion by virtue of its shape, which tends to shed water, and by the oil which is so often thrown off the prop. In fact, it tends to be the periphery of your floor which would normally cause the most concern.

10-8. Floor must be positioned accurately to supporting structures.

Boot floors can also present the same problems, with the added possibility of a pool of water in the spare wheel well.

TYPICAL MID-FLOOR REPAIR

Local repairs to rusty floors are a pretty simple affair, though you can't afford to skimp on the stripping out. Remove as much trim from the areas as possible, or

face the risk of fire damage. If you only need to patch a mid-floor hole, then cut a plate to fit the damage plus a margin for overlap, and mark this clearly onto the floor. Cut away the rotten metal and remove all underseal, paint and bituminous pad from the repair area. Underseal is best removed by heating from the inside of the car and scraping from the outside. Wear

10-9a to 10-9c. Boot floor repair.

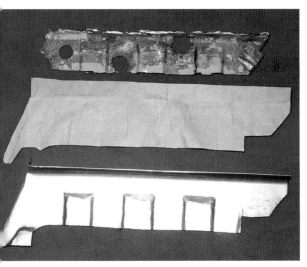

10-9a. Gash metal, template, repair section.

10-10. Beautiful boot floor section – I only put this in to show off!

10-9b. Out with the old ...

10-9c. ... and in with the new.

gloves, of course, and try to avoid applying direct heat to the underseal as this tends to cause it to melt (heating it from inside the car will tend to cause the underseal to separate from the panel). Bituminous pads are often best struck sharply with a hammer as they tend to become brittle with age. Try to avoid damage to the floor itself, though, and watch out for flying shards – wear goggles! Stubborn bits of bitumen will require heating and cleaning off with a wire brush after scraping, as will any remnants of underseal which have failed to let go. Paint is best removed with a nylon wheel on your drill or by a flap disc on the grinder. Either way, you are going to kick up some dust!

The easiest way to approach the welding is to lay the new piece over the hole and stitch around the inside before tidying up underneath. You may find that the new piece will lift off the floor as it heats, so a few well-placed PKs might help. I tend to lay a heavy hammer or a metal block on top of the patch to keep it down. You may need to dress the patch as you proceed; shaped patches will distort less than flat ones.

One very good cheat is to lay a flat patch over a swaged area and tack the new metal where it sits over the higher sections of the pressing. Then, using the support of these areas and the heat of the weld as it cools, you can dress the patch into the lower areas and continue welding. This is made even easier if, during dressing with a cross pien, a flat dolly is laid under the floor.

Installing more elaborate panel sections involves variations of the above.

Half floor sections
The important thing to watch out for when

fitting a half floor is the joint across the middle, which, ideally, would be positioned over an outrigger. Whenever possible, longitudinal joints should be placed over chassis rails.

Making floor sections
If you aren't lucky enough to have a

swager, then creative use of the vice and beating block will allow you to fabricate pretty much anything you need.

Start small and, once you have mastered the specific difficulties which hamper this aspect of panel making, you can go on to any size you wish. I've made sections up to about 300 x 900mm. As

a rule, though, if you need more than this and it's not available, then the car is probably a scrapper! Of course, this might not be true of some vehicles, and fabrication may be your only option.

Because any given piece of floor is likely to have deep flutes pressed into it, it's up to you how faithfully these

10-11a to 10-11c. Template to locate welds.

10-12a to 10-12f. Simple floor repair.

10-11a. Sound original substructures.

10-12a. Use paper template to mark as much information as possible.

10-11b. Ed uses a paper template to transfer the location of welds onto the new floor.

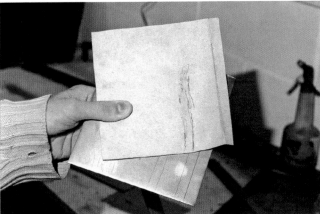

10-12b. Transferred onto metal. Marking internals may require cutting template.

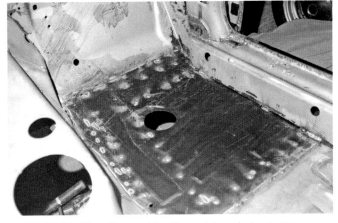

10-11c. New floor welded through to substructures.

10-12c. Working over bolster will give sharp line or step.

10-12d. Working over anvil. Cross pien used to create flute on floor.

10-12e. Floor section out ... reveals state of outrigger.

10-12f. Ready to weld.

flutes are to be reproduced. If the new piece doesn't carry the shaping on to the surrounding metal, for example, you may decide to simplify or omit some of the detail. It's more often the case that your new piece will have deep shaping on one side only. The disparity between shaped and unshaped areas will demand either stretching or shrinking.

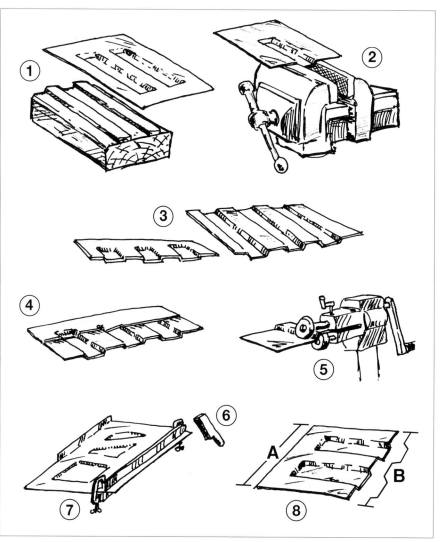

1. Wooden hammerform. 2. Use vice to form floor section. 3. Make fluted section and add end piece after. 4. BIG CHEAT! Lay flat strip and tack to top of ridges. Dress into lows. 5. Life is easier with a swager. 6. Wooden beating bat will stretch metal less. 7. Fold formed in large floor section by clamping angle iron along edge. 8. A is less than B so some stretching or shrinking is required to avoid distortion.

10-13. The extreme – you wouldn't want to make anything bigger.

Chapter 11
Multiple panel assemblies

Multiple panel assemblies, such as those found at the front end of the E-type Jaguar and many of the sporty little Triumphs, pose special problems for the restorer. Although these are really sub-assemblies of the vehicle's body, they can, to a certain extent, be considered as standalone structures. The problem with considering these units in isolation, however, will be become obvious during refitment to the main body, as they the may not match up. Ideally, you would trial fit all the pieces before committing yourself, but the sheer size and weight of many bonnet assemblies, for example, mitigates against this. As the job progresses, you'll often find it necessary to break these items down further into smaller sub-structures. You can generally expect your rebuilt front end to be a combination of new panels, new repair sections and some smaller repair patches that you'll have to make. You may often have to refit old pieces which you've previously unpicked.

11-1a & 11-1b. Localised rust allowed this bonnet assembly to be rebuilt on the vehicle.

11-1a.

11-1b.

11-1c. Typical components of bonnet assembly.

11-2. The classic 60s brute awaits attention.

11-2 to 11-25. Rebuild GT6 bonnet assembly.

11-3. Lack of detail under front suggests filler – and filler I found!

Of course, many aspects of your vehicle can be viewed as sub-assemblies (the doors, boot lid (trunk), and even the body-tub, for example), and are subject to the same problems, to a greater or lesser degree.

When working on any multi-panel assembly, try to aim for even support and symmetry of alignment. A traditional way to ensure this is to run a string along the centreline and work out from it, whilst checking with a T-square to prevent 'parallelogramming.' Vehicles with a separate chassis will allow you to use the chassis as a jig for alignment, in the horizontal plane, at least.

TRIUMPH GT6

The car featured here is a Mark I Triumph GT6 and exemplifies the sort of problems that you'll probably have to deal with. When asked to rebuild it, I budgeted a week for the job (and quoted accordingly), but I have to say it was jolly hard work! As you can see from the pictures, this car has had some dodgy repairs over the years, and a proper job was well overdue.

It's a good idea, as I've said before, to familiarise yourself with the parts catalogue, as this will help with the build order and can clarify the location and fit of parts obscured by the mists of time (and filler). Also, always wait for the new parts to arrive before you cut anything out, as you may create problems for yourself later. If you're working off the car, you'll need a good deal of space in which to work, of course, and you'll also need an assistant to help with the heavier parts. You'll need all the usual hand tools, obviously, and a spot welder will save a lot of time and produce a better job than the MIG welder, although the MIG will be needed for some repair sections. An angle grinder with appropriate discs will suffice for all the cutting, and something to rest the bonnet on will be very useful. I found that working with the assembly inverted on a table and workmate allowed free access

and lessened the amount of man-handling required (which, in turn, lessened the risk of distortion). A tape measure and some string will also prove useful. It goes without saying, of course, that you will have the appropriate safety gear.

In cases like this, you won't really know what you've got until you start to undo it. Check out the front corners, though, there's a lot of pug in that area, so you can be sure the metal underneath is pretty sad.

The first thing to do is to remove all the lamps and fittings (you're certain to uncover more horrors lurking in the water traps beneath). The wiring is generally pretty simple, but do yourself a favour and flag each piece as you disconnect it. Next, you'll have to remove the bonnet from the car for paint stripping (a dirty, smelly and often hazardous job), though of course,

you need only strip the parts that will remain. This car, like so many out there, has had a few coats of paint over the

11-4. The new bits will dictate the job to a certain extent.

11-5. Corner shows age.

11-7. Cutting off with grinder.

11-6. The lovely Elaine strips for me!

11-8. Old metal was well in need of replacement.

years, and stripping it off proved very time-consuming. Don't be surprised to find a few dents around the nose area, and remember that old filler and underseal can be removed with a heat gun (working from the 'other' side, though, so you loosen the bond rather than melt the compound).

Although the construction of each Triumph model varies in detail, they can all be thought of as being an outer shell (bonnet, wings and lamp panels), coupled to two sub-structures (the inner wheelarch bowls). The inner wheelarches are, in turn, made in two halves, joined by a simple raised flange, from which an upright stay links to the wing/bonnet seam. The outboard half is mated to the wing around the wheelarch, while the inner is bolted to the tube-work which constitutes the hinges and the cross-brace. The inner wheelarch assembly is also connected to the D-shaped, lower front corner plates along its lower front edge, and, on all but the later Spitfires, there is an upright (referred to as an inner valance), which connects the D-plate, inner wheelarch and lamp panel. As you can see from the pictures, this is the forward mounting for the hinge tubes. There are, of course, a few other minor bits and bobs.

Now that you can see what you've got, you can decide on what to replace, what to save, and what to repair. Incidentally, the only parts available to me for this model were the wing, D-plates, inner valance, repair sections for the lamp panels, and the outer half of the inner wheelarches.

I used a marker pen to define my cut lines, staying well clear of anything fiddly, but, fearing the loss of any datum point, I also thought it wise to mark precisely my joint for the lamp panel repair. This was done by simply measuring up a set amount on each side and ruling across with a flexible straight edge. Before setting-to with the cutting disc, I tidied up and removed the small front crossmember which holds the grille (while making notes for later reference), and grinding off the return edge on the rear of the wing, door-skin style.

The serious cutting is best started with the bonnet inverted. As you can see, I cut along the outside of the inner wheelarch centre seam, then, with the whole thing overhanging the table, I cut

11-10. Rebuilt arch assembly ...

11-11. ... mixes old and new.

11-9. Drilling seam with cobalt drill.

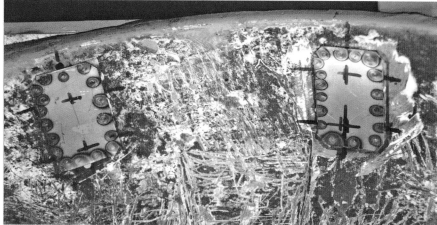

11-12. Mounting holes mapped onto patch.

11-13. Arch to bonnet – note block. Location is critical.

outside of the bonnet/wing seam and low of my joint line on the lamp panel. At this point the gash metal fell freely to the floor.

After repeating the process on the other side, I set about cleaning up the edges.

Next, I removed what was left of the wings by drilling out the spot welds and peeling off the remainder. Of course, I could have drilled these earlier (whilst still on the car, even), but it makes little difference. Before removing the stay between the inner wheelarch and the bonnet, I cut locating nicks with a hacksaw each side, top and bottom. Next, I pulled what was left of the wheelarch clear and removed the remaining metal in a similar fashion. After cleaning the flanges with a soft grinding disc, I gave them all a coat of zinc spray.

Inner wheelarch rebuild

The inner half of the inner wheelarch tends to fare better than the outer half for some reason, but only now when repairing it can you truly get the measure of the rot (mounting holes that initially appeared sound, for example, subsequently crumbled to dust). The accompanying pictures show a simple patch and hole location technique, though I would have used new units had they been available. The outer sections are nicely-made pieces and fit pretty well. They are obviously designed to be spot welded, but MIG will do if that's all you have. A small stitch on the underside at each end, and about 1in (25mm) of stitch every 3 inches (75mm) above will do. If you want it to look original,

however, then drill a million or so holes and MIG-spot them (a lot of work for little return).

Rejoining the inner wheelarch to the bonnet

Before the wings can be fitted, the connecting stay from the wheelarch must be located. Failure to align the connecting stay and the wing properly will result

in a ripple in the latter due to stresses produced as the wheelarch is pulled into place. Correct location can be achieved by refitting the cross-brace and the use of a wooden block, as in picture 11-13. Centring the drill holes will also provide a datum, but this assumes the new panels to be accurate, which so often they are not! Another approach would be to locate the wings, make the wheelarches fit, and then

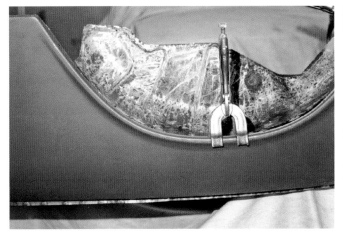

11-14. Wing to arch. Make any adjustments to the inner panel.

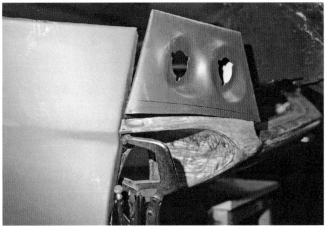

11-17. Locate and cut-in lamp panel section ...

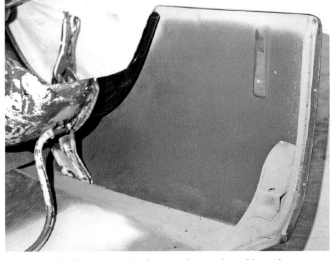

11-15. Wing rear edge is turned over doorskin style ...

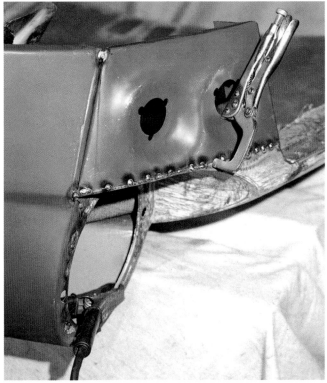

11-18. ... weld in lamp panel.

11-16. ... and front around lamp panel.

commit the stay to place and, if need be, skim off the top with a grinder!

Fitting new wings

Align the new wings to the bonnet seam and secure with as many clamps as you can. Check the fore and aft position, though this is usually governed by the headlamp panel, and, if you have to compromise it, go for a neat rear edge. The fit of this wheelarch required a bit of tweaking, but not an unreasonable amount, and I punched holes around the lip as I don't have the correct electrodes (MIG-spots will do). You should only begin welding when you're totally happy with the fit. Weld the top edge first (preferably spot, but MIG will do at a push, though it's worth drilling and plug welding), but take care not to overheat and distort the panel. Work across the job, a spot here and a spot there, allowing time for each to cool before applying heat to the same area.

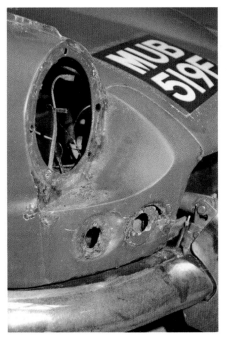

11-19. From this ...

11-21. Bodged repairs make it impossible to see the original form of the D-plate.

11-20. ... to this.

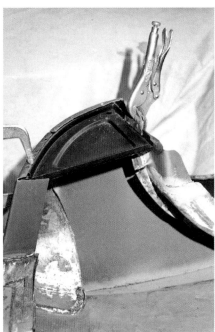

11-22. D-plate is located.

11-23. The Devil's in the detail!

Whatever technique is used, a small stitch at each end will help give a neat finish. A single spot weld at the lower rear corner is used to fix the stay, and the edge is then turned over, door-skin style (use a heavy flat dolly to prevent deflection). Complete the welding around the wheelarch and headlamp panel.

LAMP PANEL REPAIR
The lamp panel is a deep and complex 'scallop' shape, and it's prone to rust

damage around all of its seams and fittings. In addition to the supplied pieces, I had to let in a length of L-section which I'd edge-shrunk along the inside of the OS scallop. I then dealt with the scabbing around the bonnet joint by simply displacing it with MIG and facing it off with the grinder.

Although the repair sections are good quality pressings, they do need to be trimmed to size. I opted to use butt joints here, and they came out pretty well,

though you can use a joddled-lap (but trim the panels for a short butt joint at each end first, so as to get the neatest possible result).

D-PLATE & INNER VALANCE
If you look at the pictures of the car in its unrepaired state, you'll see that it gave no clues as to the original form of the D-plates. I had to refer to my magazine collection to clarify things (though the parts catalogue would also have helped).

11-25. Completed assembly – look through the lamp hole.

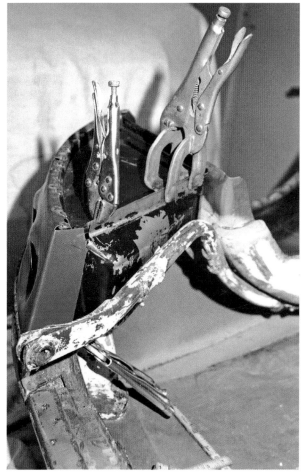

11-24. Hinge replaced to aid location.

It's a good idea to refix the hinge bars while you're setting up the inner valances, before you weld the back of the D-plates to the wheelarches. You should also support the bonnet squarely and evenly, and check across with a straight edge so as not to twist it as you build it up. In this particular case, I MIG welded the Ds to the wings and spotted to the rest.

If you have trouble aligning the wheelarch, cut the outer seam and the inner edge level with the top of the inner valance, and pry it to fit.

As you will by now realise, any misregister between the individual parts will have a knock on effect when it comes to putting the complete assembly together. You can minimise this problem by trial fitting every part with is neighbours. Reproduction inner wheelarch sections, for example, often don't mate well with their outer wheelarch counterparts, so you'd do well to tinker with the offending article before final fitment, rather than attempting to squeeze it into place, whereupon it might throw itself and the adjacent panels out of line.

The key to building up multi-panel assemblies is, as with many aspects of restoration, to always check everything twice. You'd also do well to make templates from each assembly, and also from the adjacent units, before dismantling.

As stated before, you must ensure that your work is properly and evenly supported at all times, or you will find that your assembly gets twisted. It's a good idea to have a stock of wooden blocks to hand, and an old scissor jack can be employed to support tricky items. Clamps of every type can be put to good use on this sort of job, of course, and it's often useful to tie some strong string around your assembly, and use it to pull together panels which might tend to splay outward.

Chapter 12
Wheelarches

Over the years that I've been doing this job, I've become increasingly aware that the complex process of assessing the condition of a vehicle's body can be distilled into one simple question: what are the wheelarches like?

You don't need me to tell you that wheelarches rot, of course, or that many old motors have been poorly repaired in that department. Everyone, it seems, knows the wrong way to repair a wheelarch. Fibreglass, chicken wire and polyester filler might look good for a while, but they rarely hold up for long. In many cases, this type of repair will actually compound the problem by allowing rusting to continue unchecked.

So, what's the right way to tackle your rotten wheelarch? The answer to this question will depend on several factors, such as:

Money – The more metal you disrupt the more you must paint. It'll cost more than filler!

Complexity – Is there an inner wheelarch, for example, and what has to be unpicked?

Extent – Is the affected area restricted to a localised area, is the rot light or severe, or have you got see-through wings?

Originality – You may wish to keep as much old metal as possible.

Availability – What panels are available?

THE OPTIONS
Complete panel replacement – This is probably going to be the most costly option, though what that means in real terms depends on your particular model, of course. The last time I looked, Stag rear quarter panels cost a whopping £1000 per pair for the good ones (if you can still find them). Complete rear wings for a Spitfire, on the other hand, cost £90 +VAT each (for the better ones, that is, which are worth the extra expense). Front wings for the Stag are £135 +VAT, but just £42.50 +VAT for the Spitfire.

Although your budget is an important factor, the time and effort needed to do the job (and the value of the end result, of course), are also worthy considerations. What may be a worthwhile effort on a Ferrari Dino, for example, may be time wasted on an MG Midget. This is also my rationale for buying the better quality panel, since the time spent making the poorer quality item fit is wasted money, as far as I am concerned; but that, of course, depends on how you price your time.

Half panel sections – Half panels are available for most popular models, and can represent very good value for money. For example, a top-notch half rear quarter panel for the Stag is only £80 +VAT. However, when you look at the repair sections for the front wings, the difference in price is far less, and repair may be a false economy over full panel replacement. The Spitfire rear wing is so

easy to replace that the idea of putting a seam through the middle of it appears less than sensible to me. This may or may not be true of your particular model, and it should also be pointed out that it takes a brave man to put five feet of weld through the middle of the Stag's most distinctive panel.

Arch sections – Wheelarches are widely available, and will usually represent good value for money. Quality is variable, to say the least, as some of the presses have seen better days. Even fairly sad examples, though, can be turned into perfectly presentable finished jobs with a bit of care.

Lip repair – This is one of my specialities. It's a technique that I have developed and, with a bit of care and an eye for a fair curve, you too can employ it to great effect. This method is only suitable for the wheelarch which is just starting to let go, though.

Semi-circular patch – This is another technique for those with minor or very localised rot. The method is also useful for when the rust has started to creep away from the lip.

Inner wheelarches – There is no point in opting for a minimal wing repair when half your inner wheelarch is falling out. Inner wheelarch repairs might mean anything from a blob of weld to a complete bowl. Replacing the complete bowl is usually the safest and least complicated option, assuming that the new panels are a reasonable fit. Trial fit the new inner and outer wheelarch to check the profile, and make any adjustments to the inner piece before fitting to the car. Always locate the new inner wheelarch with the outer panel in situ.

Assessment

Assessment is everything. Before you start your repair you must fully expose the true condition of the area in question. This is best done with a blow torch or (safer) with a heat gun and scraper. Since the rust is mostly caused by water sitting inside the seam and working its way out, you can't rely on what is visible from the outside. Have a bit of a pick at the damage and get a feel for what lurks behind it. As a rule, the situation is rarely better than it first appears; believe me!

REPLACING A WHEELARCH

The saloon featured here had been sitting for many years on its owner's driveway. I was asked to replace the sills and front wheelarches with parts supplied, but unfortunately the nearside wheelarch was not available.

I dealt with the offside sill first, which required opening up the bottom of the wing for access and making good. The new sill section didn't reach the full span, though, and was really of the cover-sill variety.

Next I dressed the rotten wheelarch back to something like its original shape, before offering the new piece up for comparison and rough marking with a pencil. When you're doing this, try to get as close a fit as possible; use clamps and, if need be, remove any old filler or rust which would otherwise throw the piece off-line. Also, look out for swage lines and other features which need to be aligned. Don't be afraid to chop the new panel to fit; if you only require half then fit half, or trim it so as to best control the heat distortion from the welding. You must also bear in mind the access needed if an inner wheelarch is present. Whatever you decide, trim the wheelarch before you finally mark up the wing (removing the paint will also make life easier).

It is usual to use a lap joint for this sort of repair but, again, there are decisions to be made. Watch out for the water trap with a lap joint which has the new piece under the old. Furthermore, if you're not fitting the complete section, a butt joint will have to be employed at some point to avoid the extra thickness of metal showing proud. On wheelarches with a pronounced lip, a straight butt will work as the radius of the panel will control the distortion. Panels with a flatter profile will require you to trim your new section to form a radius at the end, so as not to have

12-1. New arch *in situ*.

12-2. Old metal removed ... reveals inner arch bodge.

it go all wobbly. The butted end will run onto the lap joint.

Having decided where to cut and what joints to use, I roughly cut out the gash metal, leaving a good margin for error. I used a cutting disk on my grinder, though much of the work could have been done with a pair of snips. How you separate the inner wheelarch from the outer will depend on its condition. Drilling will be required on sound sections, so as not to move anything that might be useful for alignment later.

With the bulk of the rotten metal removed, and the inner wheelarch

dressed into some sort of shape, I refitted the new wheelarch section so as to get a final cut line. As you can see from the pictures, I used PKs to make the new piece sit flat against the old, and would advise you to do the same. However, when exactly you drill and insert them is up to you; as is how many you feel are necessary to do the job.

Having made the final cut, you might choose to joddle the edge of the receiving panel. To be honest, though, I joddled one side but not the other and the welding came out the same! This is partly due to a good choice of where to put the seam,

12-3. Forming new inner sections to fit outer is easier with the new arch off the vehicle.

12-6. New arch is fixed in with care regarding heat dissipation.

12-4. Tacking inner arch repairs using a mirror rather than craning under the car.

12-7. Wing is closed at bottom. It required a small section to be fabricated by my son, Edmund.

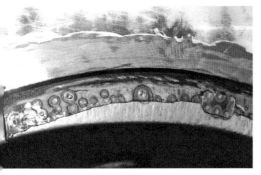

12-5. Inner repair complete. Rust protection is an issue.

partly due to good welding control, and partly due to dumb luck.

Inner wheelarch repair

As you'd expect, the inner wheelarches were a bit tatty. I found that the simplest way to deal with them was to fabricate 18mm x 18mm L-sections using the inside of the new wheelarch as a template. I teased the metal into shape by edge-spreading and cold-shrinking (see the chapter on metal forming techniques).

Fitting required that the new wheelarch be located onto the car, and then the inner wheelarch piece was clamped in place. The new inner pieces were then tacked from behind, using a mirror, then the outer wheelarch was removed and the welding completed.

Welding in the new wheelarch

As with most welding jobs on external panels, the key is to control the distortion. If the join shows or the panel warps, then your efforts will have been for nothing. Having got the new piece to fit very closely, I placed tacks of weld around the join; as usual I kept them as far apart as possible so as to allow the heat to dissipate. When the welds got to within about one inch (25mm) of each other, I filled in the gaps. In order to control the heat distortion, I worked on areas as far apart as I could.

After completing the main seam, I clamped and plug welded the new wheelarch to the inner.

With the welding completed, I first ground off the excess metal with a hard disk and then used a 36grt soft disk. When you do this, it's important to stroke rather than jab the disc, and angle it so as not to remove anything from the surrounding metal. As the excess is removed, you will encounter the odd pin hole, but these can be filled with a spot of MIG.

MAKING A NEW WHEELARCH

For some reason, only one front wheelarch was available for the car shown here, so I set about devising a practical way of producing my own. If I do say so myself, the result was pretty good, and what's more, with a little thought, this method can be used to make wheelarches for just about any vehicle you care to name, and at virtually no cost!

You will need: 2 x 1m steel rod, approx. 8mm thick (stakes used for temp fencing are ideal); a piece of heavy board, approx. 0.5m x 1m (or to fit the piece you wish to make), and a bench to place it on; template paper plus scissors, tape and pencil; sheet metal with cutting gear and clamps, PKs, etc; urethane mallet and cross pien, plus hammers and dollies as required for your specific forming requirements.

As with most jobs, you'll need to decide how much needs to be replaced. A bit of judicious hammer work will help in this, and it will also realign any bulges and bumps which, in turn, will help you to form your piece correctly.

Shape formers
These are the key to the whole operation, and are made by forming the steel rod into a copy of the wheelarch (following the line of the wheelarch in one plane only). In the case of this vehicle, with its deep brow line, I made two identical formers. For other, more shallow wheelarches, I might use only one. In fact, for a brow-less or particularly flat wheelarch, I would simply cut the curve out of the board itself and work with that. In fact, the more I think about it, the more variations and possibilities I can see.

The next step is to fix the formers to the board. How you do this will depend on the shape you are working to, of course, but you must remember that the fixings must not interfere with forming the metal.

Having decided how much of the wheelarch to make, you must now make an appropriate paper template. Masking

12-8 to 12-16. Form new arch section.

12-9. Wires fixed to board – details will vary according to specific needs.

paper is ideal for this job but, whatever paper you use, the important factors are that it will not stretch or tear, and it must not be so heavy as to prevent you from following the metal as you work it.

Stick your paper to the wing and mark the curve which you take to be the true lip of the wheelarch. This might sound odd but, because the radius of the lip may alter around the wheelarch, it's up to you to decide which line you wish to work to. It's also imperative that, having decided upon this line, the template doesn't move when marking any detail relative to it.

For ease of handling and forming, you may find it useful to make the new section (and, therefore, the template), larger then you need. Having marked up your main template with all the relevant information about the depth of the wheelarch and the position of any swages, etc, you should

now consider profile templates to ensure correct profiling and curvature. In extreme cases, you may take this information from the other side of the car and reverse it, or it may even have to come from another vehicle. You must also consider marking a datum on the template, on the former, and on the wing.

Having made the template, you must now mark and cut your metal blank. The curve of the wheelarch is the most important line and, in order to mark it correctly, you may need to sacrifice the template itself by cutting it to access inner lines. It's worth considering where on the new metal you will have to concentrate your shaping. Include as much information as possible from the template onto the metal blank, it will pay you dividends later.

Cutting the metal blank is a fairly straightforward procedure. I like the Sykes

12-8. Wire former is 'flat.'

12-10. Paper template must be securely attached ...

mini-cutter, though shears or a nibbler would do just as well.

Forming the wheelarch

Now the fun starts. The metal blank must be accurately aligned over the former, a quick check of the template might help here.

Some difficult shapes will benefit from clamps or the odd PK to stop 'sympathetic' movement. To avoid distortion of very flat sections, I'd suggest that a second wooden former be clamped over the top (see the accompanying diagram).

Using a urethane mallet, begin by breaking the edge of the wheelarch over the former. It will soon become apparent if your workpiece and former are properly aligned.

If you find the piece is tending to contract inward, then you may need be use the cross pien to stretch the inside edge. As a rule, working inside of the curve line will cause contraction, while working outside with cause expansion, so some balancing is required to keep the thing true.

Only when the inside edge has really begun to take shape, should you start to work on the area on the outside of the wing. You'll find that the inner edge will hang onto the former, thus helping to control the shaping.

I found my particular wheelarch brow took shape very quickly and easily. In fact, the work only took

about half an hour. Every wheelarch will be different, however, in both detail and method of working, so you may need to employ a dolly to help create a specific curve profile. The wheelarch you see here required only the urethane mallet and a few taps from the cross pien to ease open the inner lip. All the forming was done in situ on the former, apart from a trial fit over the existing rotten wheelarch. Profile templates can be employed to ensure accurate shaping.

You will, of course, realise that what

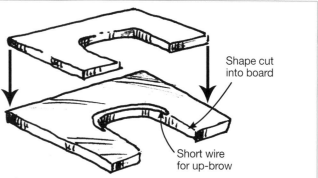

Alternative wheelarch formers, the second board on top keeps the panel flat.

12-11. ... and is then checked against former for accuracy ...

12-12. ... before transferring to metal. If need be, cut template to help mark inner lines.

12-14. Shaping with urethane mallet. Begin by tucking arch lip under.

12-13. Metal blank is located on former to check line of arch.

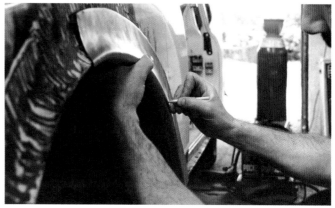

12-15. Location of shrink is marked with panel *in situ*.

you have produced so far is a 'flat' copy of your wheelarch, which will not be of any use without some tweaking to make it wrap around your wing. In order to make the new wheelarch follow the original, we simply need to insert a few cold shrinks at strategic points around the inner lip (see the chapter on Metal Forming Techniques). Very minor changes in profile can be made by simply altering the angle of the inner lip.

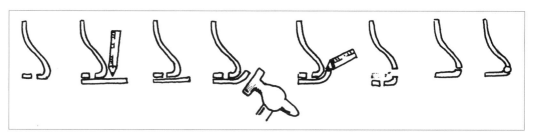

Arch lip repair – a technique suited to many of our cars.

Use of profile templates might help here, as will trial fitting. Any over-use of the shrinking technique can easily be rectified by simple application of the cross pien.

As you can see from the pictures, I have fixed the new wheelarch in place with a few PKs, which allowed me to see where adjustment was necessary and effect the alteration.

HALF ROUND REPAIR SECTION

This is a variation of the circular patch technique I am so fond of (see the chapter on Sectional Repairs). The idea is to let in a new section of metal with the minimum of distortion, and the technique is really only suited for wheelarches with severe, but very localised rot. In theory at least, though, there's no limit to the size of the new piece.

Having decided on the size and location of your repair, mark up and cut out an appropriate-sized disk from new steel sheet of the correct gauge. With the aid of a paper template, mark the line of the wheelarch and any other relevant information, and then cut and form the disk into a copy of the original damaged area. With the forming completed, lay the

new piece in place and mark around it as closely as possible.

The next step is to cut out the area to be replaced (this is probably best done by first drilling a series of holes just inside the cut line and 'nipping' between them with snips or a hacksaw blade). The resulting hole must be finished off very cleanly to ensure neat welding, which, in turn, will be dependant on a close and level fit.

During the welding process, the aim is to allow the patch to dissipate the heat as much as possible and so distort as little as possible, which is why I've used a piece of this shape.

Once the new metal is accurately fitted, you can begin welding. Place a tack at the outer points along the wheelarch line first, and then place a tack at the centre of the join (i.e. the furthest point from the previous welds). Continue tacking around the weld line, trying always to keep as far from the previous welds as possible. As you run out of space, and find your welds to be about 1in (24mm) apart, fill in the gaps with overlapping spots of MIG. Allow the work to cool as you go to prevent too much heat building up. The underside of the wheelarch should receive drilling and stud-welding only after the outer areas are complete.

When the welding is complete grind-off with a soft disk, and skim with filler as required (you should also refer to the chapters on sectional repairs and doors).

ARCH LIP REPAIR

I consider this technique my own, and have used it to save many a panel from replacement. Although it's mainly suited to areas of localised rotting, so many wheelarches begin corroding along the lip that quite a few vehicles will be candidates for repair by this means. The aim is to is surgically replace the lower lip of the wheelarch by cutting-in a new piece along the bottom edge.

12-17a to 12-17j. Lip repair.

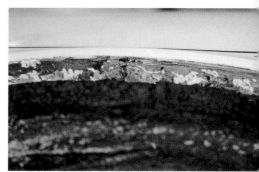

12-17a. Attack of the tin worm.

As usual, the first thing to do is to assess the damage. It's no use employing this method if you require extensive work to an inner panel, as you won't have the necessary access. Therefore, the first step is to decide how much to replace, and then dress the area back to as original a shape as possible.

Having decided how much of your wheelarch to replace, you must now decide how many pieces you wish to replace it with. For a full wheelarch I would recommend three pieces. You can do it in one hit, of course, but I find this method to be very wasteful of metal, and brings with it a lot of unnecessary hassle, with no advantage.

TEMPLATES

For a complete wheelarch, cut three strips of card approx. 300mm x 75mm. The

12-16. Arch is ready for welding. Note butt joint at front.

width (300mm) is dependant on the profile and thickness of your particular wheelarch.

Hold each piece in place and roughly mark the shape of the wheelarch onto the card. Be sure to fix a datum and mark each piece against its neighbour. Overlap the sections and mark up for butt jointing, then transfer the information onto new steel sheet and cut out.

The next step is to closely position the new metal. Use as many clamps as you can, and concentrate on matching the inner edge as best you can. The metal will take up the curve of the wheelarch as you clamp it, though you may choose to impart some of this shape by hand before locating the metal. Be careful not to mar the new metal with clamp marks, though. If necessary, lightly dress the new piece around the wheelarch with a urethane mallet, as it's important that the original shape be followed as closely as possible.

Once the new metal is clamped in place, mark a cut line on it. Ideally, you should aim for the apex of the radius, though you'll need to make sure you take

in all of the damage, so go above this if need be. Use a sharp pencil square-on to the metal, run it against the wheelarch and, if necessary, take it slightly wide so as to encompass more new metal as required.

Remove the new metal sections, re-cut along the line you've just marked, and replace your new metal, taking care to locate it exactly as before (refer to your datum).

Next, use a bumping hammer to lift the outer edge of the new metal to meet the old. Run the hammer around the wheelarch, starting with light blows from about 45 degrees below the horizontal, then progress to hammering so that the blows are connecting horizontally. If necessary, use your cross pien to spread the metal in any tight areas, but be careful not to spread the metal too thin, as this will make welding difficult.

Remove the new metal and clean the outer edge which is bound to have become a touch ragged. A file will usually suffice for this, though odd lumps can be nipped off with snips. After any

disturbance to the edge, be sure to replace and redress it.

Having achieved a decent shape and edge, mark this on the car as a cut-line with a scribe, or with masking tape (tape is easier to see when using a grinder).

Remove old metal

Remove the new sections (again), and carefully split off the gash metal with a cutting disk on your grinder. Ideally, this job would be done with a fine disk on a high speed saw or with an oscillator, but I wouldn't expect you to have access to such specialist tools. Drill out any spot welds you find inside the wheelarch, and clean the inner wheelarch as required. On some old vehicles, you'll find that a line of mastic has been interfaced between the

12-17e. Taped cut line is easier to see when using a grinder.

12-17b. Fresh steel strips closely follow around the arch...

12-17f. Removing gash metal with care after cutting.

12-17c ... are marked, and cut to allow lip radius ...

12-17d. ... and dressed to fit in situ.

12-17g. New metal in situ.

inner and outer wheelarches. This must be removed to prevent it falling like 'napalm' during the next stage of the process. Give the whole area a coat of zinc spray once it's been cleaned.

Fix the new metal

Once you've removed the gash metal, you might find that your new piece sits slightly differently than before, and might need a minor tweak or bump to give you the perfectly level join that is required.

Take great care with the welding, and make certain that the new metal aligns closely with the old before joining. Because the material on both sides of the join tends to be quite thin, you should set your welder to its minimum setting.

Begin your weld by putting a tack at each end of your repair section, then one in the middle, and then gradually build up the spaces in between, making sure not to allow the heat to build up as this might lead to distortion. You may find that the occasional tap is required to keep your seam closed. When your tacks reach to within about 1in (24mm), of each other, fill between them with overlapping spots of MIG. The inside edge of the wheelarch should be drilled and stud welded after the lip has been finished.

With the welding complete, grind off the excess metal with a soft disk on your grinder. Watch out for the metal discolouring, which is a sign of overheating, as this suggests that it's getting thin.

This technique should leave your 'new' wheelarch ready for priming, without the need for filler.

FULL REAR QUARTER PANEL/ REAR WING REPLACEMENT

Replacing a full rear quarter panel or rear wing may seem a fairly daunting task but, in essence, it's the same as changing a front wing. I say 'in essence' because, although the principals are the same, your rear quarter panel is likely to be quite a large panel, and your car's designers probably didn't figure on it ever being renewed. Furthermore, if your vehicle has a roof, then you'll also have to put in a pillar joint or two.

Pictures 12-18a to 12-18m outline the process for replacing simple rear wings, whereas pictures 12-19a to 12-19g show the procedure for more complex items.

In its simplest form, the rear wing is a panel that has been spot welded around its periphery. Removal is best accomplished by drilling out the welds. To replace the wing, the front edge must be drilled or punched to allow MIG welding to the B-post. Trial fitting with the door in situ is essential, as many examples will try to rotate under their own weight.

12-17h. Welding in progress. A tight radius is not very prone to distortion.

12-17i. After grinding the arch is looking good.

12-17j. The finished job – the repair should be invisible.

12-18a to 12-18m. Replace full RQP.

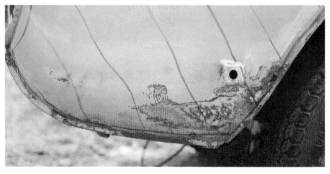

12-18a. It's got to go, as a cheap new panel makes repair a false economy.

12-18b. Drilling top seam – try not to hole-through.

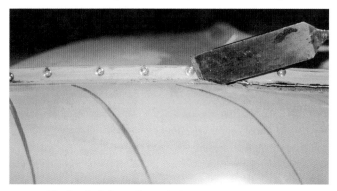

12-18c. Splitting off panel – keep your chisel sharp.

12-18d. Exposed! The ugly truth.

12-18e. Inner arch is removed and ready for the new item.

12-18f. Inner arch trial fit. It pays to check before welding.

12-18g. The inner arch fitted and ready for a new wing.

12-18h. New RQP trial fitted. Nearly there ...

12-18i. Welding top with spot welder ...

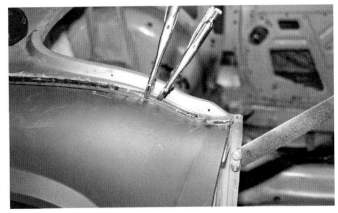

12-18j. ... the front with MIG.

12-18k. Welding the rear around the lamp panel ...

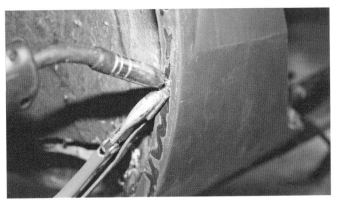

12-18l. ... and around arch with MIG again ...

12-18m ... and done. A quick grind off and no filler!

12-19a to 12-19g. More complex RQP.

12-19a. Panel comes off – note arch repair, adjacent panels and location.

12-19b. Inner arch out. Original red oxide is a good sign.

12-19c. Inner arch in. Align inner to outer.

12-19d. Check door gap. Time spent now is well invested.

12-19e. Check boot and tonneau gaps. Don't weld until it's right!

12-19f. B-post seam ready for welding – note PKs. If need be, dress seams to achieve best fit.

12-19g. Over the years, doorskin quality has varied. This door has been built up along its rear edge – why?

Always begin by aligning the panel from the door, before concentrating on the top edge and rear panel fit. Use any swage or feature lines to confirm the height, and trial fit the rear lights before you commit to welding. If your rear wing borders the boot aperture then this must be trial fitted also. Creative use of clamps, rivets and PKs will allow complete proof of correct positioning without interfering with the shut of the adjacent panels.

Concealed welds, brazed joints, etc

More sophisticated designs will usually incorporate concealed seams and the odd brazed joint in the boot aperture or where the roof is met. You might wish to 'sweat out' the brazing, but I tend to simply cut the joint and grind off the remaining braze (carefully, though, because any remnants will 'spit' when welded).

Where possible, try to reproduce the original finish of all the seams. If this is not practical, however, due to the original build order, for example, then you'll have to 'fake' the seam by MIG welding, with overlapping spots, and then facing-off with a skim of filler and a fake seam line. Alternatively, floating braze into the seam will produce a reasonable joint, though the risk of panel distortion is greater with this method. You may find that a reasonable compromise is to tack the outside of the seam with dot of MIG at strategic points, before joining the panels from behind. The outer MIG will prevent the joint from flexing, while the concealed weld, which can be spotted through pre-punched holes, will do the real work.

PILLAR JOINTS

Fixed-head vehicles usually demand that at least one pillar joint be employed if the entire panel is not to be fitted (which is normal). Similarly, the new rear quarter panel may originally have run into the sill. After the 1970s, many vehicles incorporated a 'ring-side,' which is to say that the outer face of the sill, the A and B posts, the rear quarter panel and a section of roof member were pressed as one panel. The name 'ring,' of course, refers to the complete door aperture. This system of construction continues today, often with the rear quarter panel extending into the exterior of the roof.

Anyhow, the point is that you're not going to unpick your roof for the sake of some rust around your rear wheel wheelarch, so the new panel has to be cut-in somewhere. In choosing exactly where to place your join, you must consider not only the strength aspect, which includes regard to any internal panels, but you must also allow for finishing off the join neatly, and have access for any power tools required to this end. If you intend to remove any excess MIG with a 4¹⁄₂in (115mm) grinder, then you'll need a bit more space than if you are to employ a mini power file.

INTERNALS

Panels which take in the front face of the B-post will usually incorporate some internal detail in order to locate and hold the door striker or latch pin. The exact nature will vary from model to model, while the necessary platework may or may not have to be salvaged from the original. Fitting a new body side panel, and then realising that the lock is missing, would not be so funny. Pay close attention to such things before committing yourself to welding. Internal details (including wiring), are also a consideration when making the cuts. The ideal tool for the job is an oscillator (a circular saw which oscillates rather than rotates), which allows a lot of control over the blade so very shallow and precise cuts can be performed. I tend to

use an air saw, though you can make do with a hacksaw and a cutting disk on your grinder. The less precise your tool, the greater your need for control.

While some will tell you that butt joints are desirable to get flush joints, I would always specify a stepped lap joint, with splits cut into the receiving piece to allow a flush fit. The stepped joint allows for greater flexibility without compromising strength (see the accompanying diagram).

THE INNER WHEELARCH & LOCATION

If the original inner wheelarch is still in situ, then this will dominate the location process as regards any rear wing or quarter panel. If your new panel is an accurate copy or an original, then the existence of the inner wheelarch will be a great help. However, as so many of the available panels are less than perfect, you may find the need to tweak the inner wheelarch to allow everything to sit comfortably. An inner wheelarch is generally more amenable to being tweaked than the average rear wing. Likewise, if a new inner wheelarch is to be fitted, you should align it to the new outer panel rather than vice versa.

HALF PANEL SECTIONS

Some vehicles of the 1950s and 1960s were built with a seam running through the middle of the rear quarter panel. The MGB and the Triumph Herald are good examples of this, and owners of such models are, therefore, able to renew half a rear wing without breaking from originality.

Access to the full length of the seam is not readily possible with a spot welder, though, and some compromise will have to be found.

For the majority of us, though, fitting a half section means running up to six feet of weld through one of our car's most distinctive panels without it showing.

Half panel sections can offer brilliant value for money. The rear quarter panel of the Triumph Stag, for example, is a large panel with some very distinctive compound curves, and is very prone to rusting. However, the price difference between complete and sectional panels easily justifies the use of this method of repair. However, the huge weld seam required demands great care and patience if gross distortion is to be avoided.

The new panel comes as a raw pressing, complete with a ragged edge. You'll have to spend some time fettling in order to have something that you can actually work with, but you will end up with the correct amount of new metal for your job.

With the new panel cut to size, it must now be sighted over the old wing. In order to allow the new piece to sit closely, the old metal immediately above the sill is removed or opened. The wheelarch will usually locate the new piece, though any bulging around the lip may throw the panel off line. Dress the wheelarch back into shape if need be.

A half dozen (or more) well placed screws, within ¹⁄₂in (13mm) of the top edge, will be of enormous help with the location process, and can always be

12-20. RQP is made ready for half panel section.

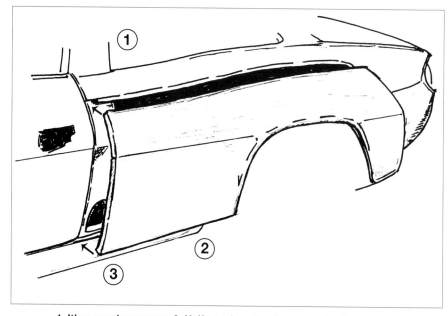

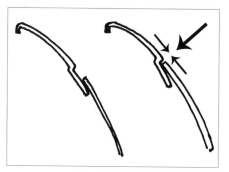

Location is critical. Pressure will cause distortion.

1. It's a very long seam. 2. Half panel section is great value for money. 3. Door gap is critical.

referred to in the event of any adjustment being made. Screw them up tightly to close the panels together.

Don't be tempted to rip out the old wheelarch, or large amounts of old gash metal, as it can be very helpful to locate the new piece over the original in order to get the profile correct (see the accompanying diagram).

Once the new section has been aligned and marked correctly, it can then be removed and the old scrap cut out (using snips, nibbler, air saw, pad saw, mondex, or even a jig saw).

Be aware of internal structures and wiring, though, as well as the fact that many rear quarter panels have bituminous pads which will clog-up your tools. This material is best removed by heating from the outside and scraping from the inside of the wing.

With the scrap removed, the vehicle must be prepared for the installation of the new section. All weld seams must be tapped up as required, and every last trace of old weld removed. Then the edge of the cut line must be 'joddled' to accept the new metal, without it sitting proud. At the front edge of this seam, where it meets the door aperture, it's usually necessary to have a short section of butt joint, as the tool used for joddling can't be used here because of the internal structures of the B-post.

With the old metal no longer supporting the new, it would be easy to set the top edge in the wrong position which, in turn, would set up uneven stresses as the welding progressed. This would result in rippling, and would be a major headache for the man who has to fill the joint prior to painting. This is why I always use PKs for location, since replacing the screws will close the panels tightly for neat welding, and will prevent any riding-over when pressure is applied.

WELDING
Heat dissipation and distortion control are paramount during the welding process. Begin by tacking at strategic points around the panel, beginning with the door aperture top and bottom, then the rear of the sill/ front of the wheelarch. Concentrating then on the big seam, aim your welds into the slight hollow that exists where the panels meet, and remember that you need a sound fusion of the old and new after the excess has been removed (see the accompanying diagram). Place tacks around the seam, keeping them as far apart as is possible. When you have reached the point where the welds are about 1 1/2in apart, fill in the gaps with overlapping spots (again, working in areas as far apart as possible). Pay special attention when running new weld onto old, as this doesn't always flow as smoothly as you might expect it to. With the welding completed, the excess must first be ground off with a hard disk, and then with a soft or flap disk. A light touch must be employed if the excess and only the excess is to be removed.

Extra control of the heat dissipation can be gained by use of a damp cloth between bursts of welding. Alternatively, a copper or steel billet pressed behind the panel can be used to absorb excess heat while also preventing the metal from sinking, which is its natural tendency.

The position of the seam is another factor in controlling the distortion, flatter areas, for example, will wobble more than curved ones. Also, bear in mind the need to use filler, as this will influence your choice of location of joint also (see the accompanying diagram).

However you tackle the job, remember that taking your time now will save wasting it later!

Chapter 13
Metal forming techniques & panel beating

BASIC METAL FORMING TECHNIQUES

The first two methods will alter the 2D shape of the flat sheet into a 3D form, though the surface area of the metal is not added to or reduced by any appreciable degree.

Folding

To some extent, the size of the project you can undertake is determined by your capacity to bend sheet metal. For example, I have for some time wanted to make a new door skin for my Anglia, but my box folder will only form folds up to 1 metre, and the door is 40in long. Box folders (metal brakes), are available in a variety of sizes, and those of 12in (300mm) tend to be reasonably priced (anything over this will cost serious money). My own machine is of the rising beam type and would have cost thousands of pounds had I not bought it for peanuts from a bodyshop which no longer wanted it. The advantage of a folding machine is that the pressure is applied evenly along the fold line, therefore producing a bend which is straight. The same length of fold, if formed by hand, might tend to warp due to the relatively small face of the hammer.

The simplest way to form a bend in a piece of steel sheet is with a vice. By clamping the work piece up to the fold line and dressing with a hammer or mallet, short bends of up to 90 degrees are easily formed. Smaller folds can be made using flat welding clamps, either in pairs or singularly. Lengthier folds can be formed over a straight edge, which might be fixed to a bench or clamped to the workpiece itself.

Note! Mark fold lines with a soft pencil or tape as the use of a scriber might cause the metal to split during folding.

Curving or rolling

Forming an even curve in your sheet may be as easy as taking hold of each end and pulling it around to the desired arc. Once you've overcome the natural limit of elasticity, your metal will hold its new shape. During a restoration job, however, it's more likely that you'll find yourself dressing your workpiece over a suitable piece of tube or rod. Again, the scope of your projects will be governed by how large a piece you can handle. Old-fashioned rolling machines are a thing of the past, and, again, I saved mine from a dumpster. T-stakes are very useful for forming curved edges and can easily be made (or expensively bought).

When dressing a piece of metal around a former, use direct (solid) blows from a soft mallet or wooden bat to mould the piece exactly around the former. Alternatively, you can aim indirect or glancing blows ahead of the former to produce a softer curve.

Shrinking & stretching

As the terms suggest, the following two techniques not only alter the shape of the metal, but will also increase or lessen the surface area. You would do well to practice these methods, as they crop up regularly and are the basis of many others.

To practice, start by cutting some 20swg steel into 6in x 1in (150 x 150mm) pieces, and then fold lengthways to produce an L-section. Your pieces should be true and straight in all planes, and you'll observe that adding metal to or subtracting metal from one face, will cause the other to curve, and that's what we intend to do.

Edge spreading

Place your L-section strip on a beating block and run blows with a cross pien up and down one face, at right angles to the workpiece. Move the metal while keeping the hammer in the same position relative to the anvil. Allow the head of the hammer to strike with the shaft horizontal. Don't try to 'punch' the metal, though, as it may split, and remember that the steel will work-harden and become brittle after a lot of hammering.

From time to time you'll have to lightly dress the workpiece with a mallet, or tap it with a hammer shaft, to overcome a natural twisting tendency. Pinching the dressed edge in the vice would also help to keep things the correct shape.

Narrow edges will spread far more easily than deep ones and, in all cases, the outermost portion of the edge will need to spread further than the area inboard.

Cold-shrinking

This is obviously the opposite of the previous exercise, and is a little more tricky, but well worth learning. Shrinking machines are available, of course, but they're not as versatile as this technique.

Start by raising a few peaks on the face to be shrunk by striking sharply with a cross pien over a slightly open vice. Remember that stretching the metal would be counterproductive, and that you are limited to how many shrinks you have room for in any length of metal and at any one time. Next, you have to manhandle the work so as to exaggerate the curve and sharpen the peaks. This is best done using a metal billet, though the end of a tube will suffice.

Now comes the tricky bit. Use the cross pien to 'tuck in' around the peaks. This is to stop the bend from spreading out again during the next step, and requires a steady hand.

Finally, flatten the peaks into themselves using several light blows, the first of which should strike from the inside of the curve at about 30 degrees. The idea is to drive the metal into itself rather than to crimp it.

To really get the hang of these two techniques, work to a template, and form a compound piece which is spread on one face and shrunk on the other.

13-3a to 13-3d. Cold-shrinking and edge spreading – a real application.

13-3a. Raising peaks. Do not stretch the metal ...

13-3b. ... form over billet and exaggerate the peaks.

13-1. Cold-shrinking exercise. Tricky, but worth learning.

13-2. Edge spreading exercise – an invaluable technique.

13-3c. Drive the metal into itself. Flatten peaks to shrink ...

13-3d. ... and spread other face. Take care not to make the piece brittle. See the sectional repairs chapter to see where the new piece goes.

THE SHRINKER/STRETCHER MACHINE & HOT-SHRINKING TECHNIQUES

The traditional hammer techniques of cold-shrinking and edge-spreading are key skills, and something every panel beater must master. Thickening and thinning the metal is fundamental in every aspect of panel formation and repair. Within the coachbuilding and custom panel fabrication industries you will find a wide variety of power-hammers and shrinking devices. The small shrinker/stretcher from Frost has been popular with body shops and home restorers for some time, and costs in the region of £200. This machine can be put to good use to help produce many of the typical panel sections you will need to restore the average classic car. While the small flat jaws and shallow throat will limit the scope of what it can handle, what it does it does do very well. An advantage of the machine over manual methods is that the worked edge remains more even in thickness, which in turn makes it easier to weld and less likely to burn or melt. In practice, you may find that the edge of a seemingly flat panel will benefit from a few very minor shrinks, or it can be used to de-stress a section of floor to iron out the odd kinks that tend to form where shaped and unshaped areas meet.

In use:

The shrinker/stretcher machine can be bolted to a bench or mounted in a vice; alternatively a proprietary stand can be purchased.

The device comes with two sets of jaws for the different jobs. Changing the jaws takes seconds and requires no tools.

I am using a piece of 20swg mild steel that has been formed into an L-section to illustrate what the machine can do.

Place the L-section into the jaws and pull the handle. You will see the jaws contract, and the metal be pulled around. The effect, though not huge with any single pull, is immediate. You may find that when working a deep flange, it pays to set the second run of shrinks (or stretches) halfway out of the jaws, as this is where the effect should naturally occur.

13-4. Shrinker/stretcher jaws.

13-5. Exercise piece in shrinker jaws.

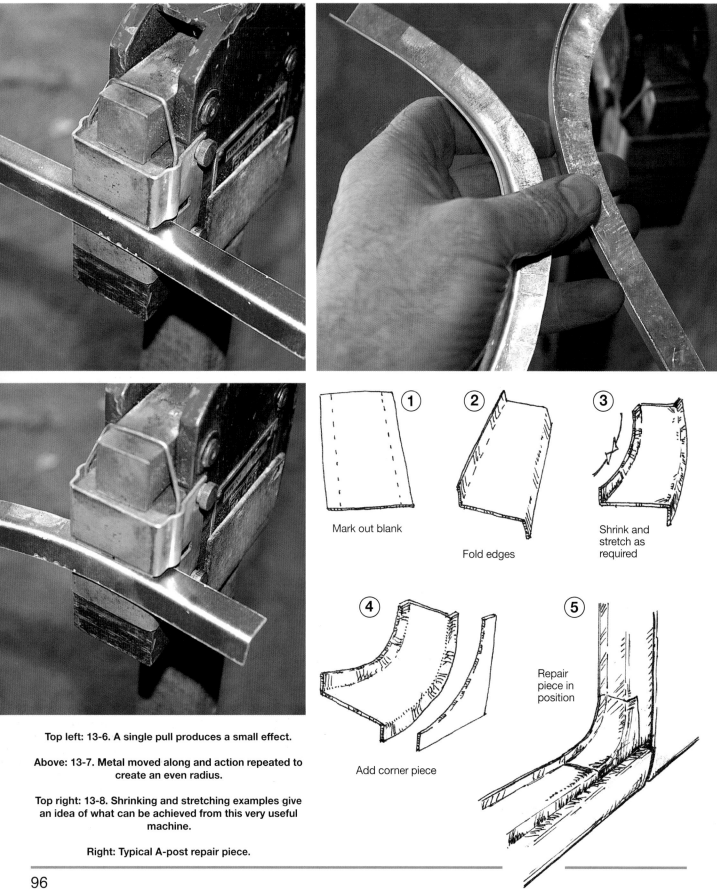

Top left: 13-6. A single pull produces a small effect.

Above: 13-7. Metal moved along and action repeated to create an even radius.

Top right: 13-8. Shrinking and stretching examples give an idea of what can be achieved from this very useful machine.

Right: Typical A-post repair piece.

① Mark out blank

② Fold edges

③ Shrink and stretch as required

④ Add corner piece

⑤ Repair piece in position

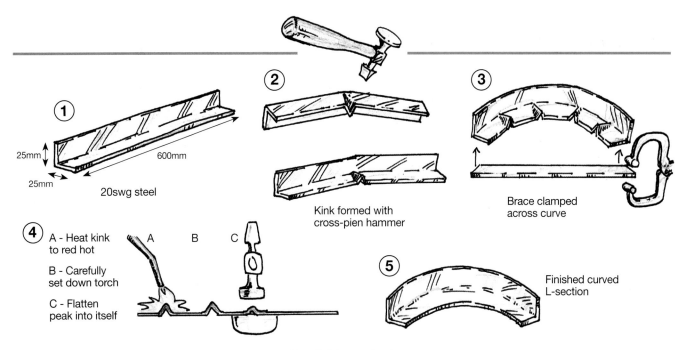

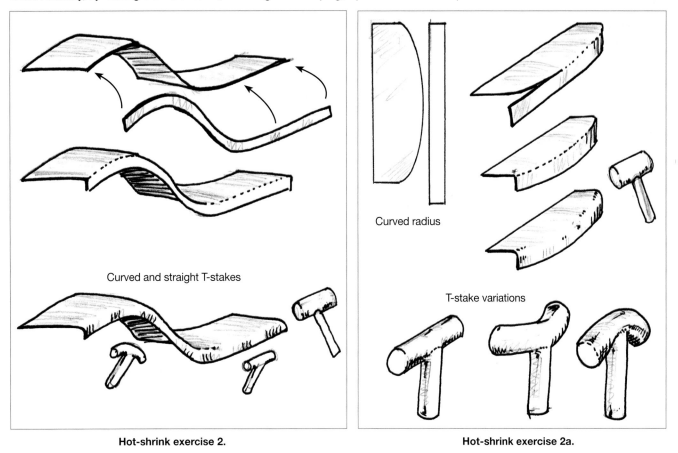

① 25mm 25mm 600mm 20swg steel

② Kink formed with cross-pien hammer

③ Brace clamped across curve

④ A - Heat kink to red hot
B - Carefully set down torch
C - Flatten peak into itself

⑤ Finished curved L-section

Hot-shrink exercise 1.

Hot-shrink exercise 1

This technique (shown above) is similar in principal to the cold-shrink method, except that it obviously involves heat! The aim is to thicken the edge by driving the metal into itself, but because the heat has softened the steel, it should be easier to work. Naturally, by making the metal softer,

there is some risk that injudicious use of the hammer could have the opposite effect. For this reason, I recommend using a boxwood mallet in conjunction with a flat dolly rather than a bumping hammer, which would be the choice of the more experienced practitioner. To control the degree of shaping, a piece of bar is

clamped across the span. This counters the tendency for the curve to open out.

An oxyacetylene or blow-torch can be used to heat the metal, which should be warmed to a bright cherry red. Wear gloves and take great care where you direct the torch during the shrinking process.

Curved and straight T-stakes

Hot-shrink exercise 2.

Curved radius

T-stake variations

Hot-shrink exercise 2a.

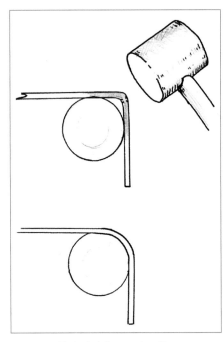

Hot-shrink exercise 2b.

Hot-shrink exercise 2

This is a fairly advanced panel fabrication technique that will need a bit of practice before being used in earnest. Once you have mastered it you will never look at a flying wing or running-board in the same light again.

This method is used in the accompanying images with the oxyacetylene gear. It works equally well with TIG (which is probably safer) and can be employed at a push with MIG.

You will also need a boxwood mallet or bumping hammer and an appropriate T-stake.

SAFETY

These heat-shrinking methods involve heavy cumbersome equipment and very hot metal that needs to be handled very carefully. In both techniques, the torch will have to be set aside while the shrinking process takes place. The need to work quickly will often tempt you to lay the torch down while it is still lit, which is hugely dangerous, especially while your attention is elsewhere. Never attempt to hold a lit torch between your knees. Invest in a torch stand or better still, commandeer an assistant.

PLANISHING, RAISING, & HOLLOWING

These are the methods by which we form crowns and compound curves in sheet metal.

Planishing

Planishing is a hammering technique which involves the workpiece being moved over a dolly or stake while being beaten evenly with a smooth-faced hammer. By striking directly (solidly) the surface finish of both the dolly and the hammer will be imparted onto the work. Traditionally, pieces which have been formed by raising and hollowing are given their final finish by this means. Planishing can also be employed to form shapes, for example, bowls and spoons, and is usually the first technique to be taught. Planishing can also be carried out using a wheeling machine, though these devices are few and far between in the modern bodyshop. Whether by hammer or wheel, it's important that planishing be carried out with great care, so as not to stretch the piece out of shape. Planishing will also tend to work-harden the item, which may leave it brittle and in need of annealing.

Hollowing

Hollowing is a method of forming bowls or crowns in sheet metal by beating the workpiece against a sandbag or hollowed wooden log. Traditionally, the beating is carried out with a pear-shaped wooden mallet, a heavy rubber mallet or a steel round head hollowing hammer. While the wood and rubber tools will tend to draw the sheet into shape, the heavy steel hammer will tend to have more of a stretching effect. To make a bowl using this technique you'd normally start working from the outside edge and rotate the piece while striking evenly overlapped blows, which you would continue in concentric circles toward the centre or base.

Working in this fashion will tend to cause the outer regions of the bowl to pucker unevenly, which must be addressed to avoid pointing and cracking. The puckered excess metal is shrunk by forming the raised area into a peak. By aiming a blow either side of it, this will tend to control the effect of the next set of blows which are worked from the outside of the bowl inward. These are intended to smooth and shrink the metal in a similar manner to the previous cold-shrink exercise.

Raising

Raising is the method by which we shape sheet metal around a dolly or former from the outside using a mallet or hammer. This technique differs from planishing in that the aim is to draw the metal into shape rather than pinch it between former and hammer. In practice, using this method to form bowls will cause puckers in the same way as hollowing, which will then need to be shrunk back and smoothed. It's usual to finish the piece by planishing.

SPLIT & WELD – A MODERN TAKE ON PANEL FORMATION

The traditional metal forming techniques of raising, hollowing and planishing have stood the panel beater in good stead for generations. While these methods work, and work well, they can sometimes be usurped by the young upstart which is 'split and weld' to great effect.

Split and weld, as the name suggests, is where excess material is simply cut out, or if more material required, it is sewn in. And as my terminology suggests, the process is not unlike needlework in its philosophy. Gussets, fillets, and darts all feature here, and by using these techniques very rapid progress can be made without the risk of metal fatigue and thinning associated with more traditional working.

13-9. This tank is fabricated from at least seven sections – where would you join them?

Split and weld techniques work best with gas or TIG welding, as these methods can produce pure fusion butt welds, unlike MIG, which by its nature, deposits new material at the site of joining. However, because MIG is so common within the restoration fraternity, I have used it in the accompanying examples.

Using the MGB front valance as an example, consider how we had previously calculated the amount of shrinkage required and had seen where material needed to be lost using the paper template. With these older methods of working, it was then necessary to shrink the metal surface by beating it into itself – a skilled and inherently slow process. (But none the less well worth learning.)

Employing the split and weld technique, the paper is used to rationalise where best to remove the excess metal, which is marked and then chopped out surgically. The sides are then pulled together and the seam stitched with weld. Hammering is often useful to relieve stresses and to help align the edges, either before or immediately after welding. Hammering after welding whilst the join is still hot – known as hammer welding – helps to reinstate surface tension and makes the shaping easier.

Adding material in a similar manner, as opposed to working the metal thinner and thinner to produce a deep hollow, has benefits in that the metal will not become brittle and is not at risk of splitting.

Most vehicles have panels originally produced using a 100 tonne press. Such machines can produce very deep drawing, or indeed press a panel in several stages. Using just our hammers we have little or no chance of replicating this degree of draw or many of the complex shapes from a single piece of 20swg steel.

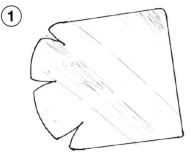

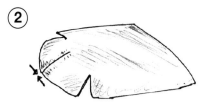

Metal blank is rationalised using paper or card templates

Manhandle the blank so that the sides of the split close together. Judicious use of a mallet may be of help here

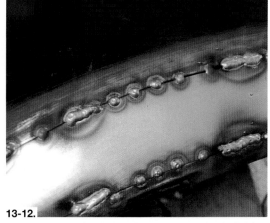

Slits are carefully welded, and excess removed

Mallet and dolly used to even out the shape and reinstate surface tension

Split and weld procedure.

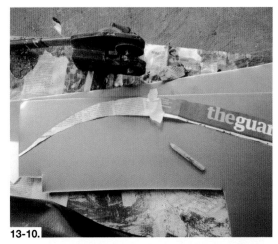

13-10.

13-11.

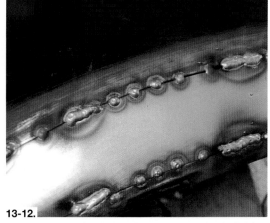

13-12.

13-13.

Split and weld techniques should not be considered as replacements for more traditional methods, but as complimentary alternatives to them. The more weapons we have in our arsenal, the more we can achieve. Cold- and hot-shrinking, along with the surgical removal or insertion of new metal, can allow us to produce rare and beautiful metalwork, which in turn can mean that more of our classics will survive.

13-10. Paper template is traced onto steel to make the fillet.
13-11. New fillet is shaped by hand and set in panel carefully.
13-12. Tack weld the new section with care so as not to distort the panel.
13-13. New arch contour is seamless.

Chapter 14
Basic hammer exercises

You might assume from reading the previous section that creating a bowl or crown from sheet metal requires the use of specialist and expensive equipment, such as dolly heads and sandbags. This is not the case, however, and it is possible to create a large bowl from a standard round dolly, for example, or even a 6mm deep hollow cut into a wooden log.

PLANISHING

The rule for planishing or metal finishing is that a flat faced hammer is used for crowned surfaces and a crowned hammer for flat. This is to control or limit the amount of surface contact. In practice, however, many panel men use only crowned hammers, and they do alright!

For this exercise you will need: sheet metal, a ruler, dividers, snips, a scribe, a round dolly and a light bumping hammer. You'll also need a vice with soft jaws and an anvil.

First, cut a piece of 20swg steel into a 6in x 6in square (150 x 150mm), then find the centre and mark a circle 4in (100mm) across. From this you will raise a bowl with a maximum depth of $1/2$in (13mm). Next, you will need two strips of metal, each 6in x $1\frac{1}{2}$in (150 x 40mm), for your template. Before you cut them out, however, you must mark them with your chosen internal

14-1. Planishing exercise. Blank template and tools.

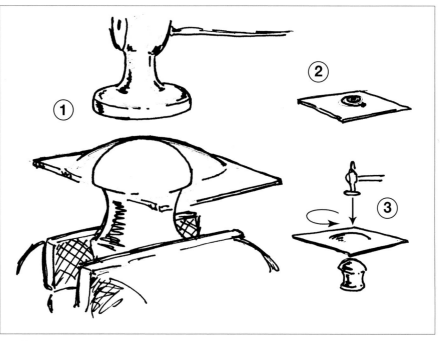

Hammer exercises – Planish. 1. Dolly held in vice. 2. Work from centre spiral out. 3. Hammer and dolly remain still while workpiece is moved around.

14-2a & 14-2b. Checking former against work.

14-2a.

14-2b.

radius. Once you've cut the template pieces out, cross-half them and fix together with a single tack.

Clamp your round dolly into your vice and position the workpiece so that the centre of the circle is over the centre of the dolly. Now, with a light bumping hammer, strike the centre of your proposed bowl.

You will immediately see the pock mark left by the blow, and will have felt and heard the hammer making contact with the dolly. It may take you a while to visualise the centre of the dolly and, therefore, consistently strike 'solid' blows. Having established the centre, tap a ring of blows around it (and then repeat this in concentric passes), and you will soon see your bowl rising out of the flat sheet. You may notice that the outer area of your square is starting to show signs of tension as the hammered rings near the outside of your circle. As the bowl progresses and the flat area becomes wobbly, lay the flat areas against your anvil or beating block (with the bowl downward and butted against one edge), and rotate the workplace while lightly defining the edge between flat and bowled areas. Remember that the flat area should not need any direct hammering as it should not be stretched, though you can get away with a few blows from a soft mallet to normalise things.

Repeat this process until your template fits the bowl in any position.

With this degree of planishing you should not require any annealing and, if you've got the hang of things (which you should), then your piece will have a smooth finish.

RAISING & HOLLOWING
Use aluminium for the purposes of this exercises, even if you intend to work exclusively in steel for real jobs. The first step is to anneal the aluminium (see below) before beating, then make internal and external templates, as these will show the principles (and problems) to good effect.

The teardrop bowl
This odd-shaped bowl might be thought of as a power bulge or air scoop, complete with mounting flange. Mark up the metal from the plan (see accompanying diagram), and make your internal and external templates from the other drawings. I have deliberately omitted the information needed to make stations for points B & C, and will leave it to your

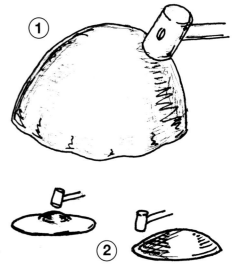

Hammer exercises – raise. 1. Like raising the work will tend to pucker at edge. 2. When raising, work from the centre outwards.

judgement as to how the shape will flow (a sensible approach might be, for example, to take a section of the radius at point A).

Cut out the metal blank and true the edges to remove any burrs or ragging. The metal can be cut with snips, a jigsaw, or a mini-cutter.

Start by hollowing into the blank with a suitable hammer (beginning at the outside and working towards the centre, of course). I prefer to begin with a heavy ball pin, but you might be a little more cautious. The uneven embossing of the ball pin can then be smoothed out by using a mallet over a round dolly. This will allow you to see the true extent of the shaping so far, as will frequent checking against the templates.

The flange might pose a problem because, as the job progresses, it may get wobbly and need to be tidied up. Be careful not to stretch the flange, though. Pinching the flange in a vice might help, as will a few mallet blows against a beating block or anvil.

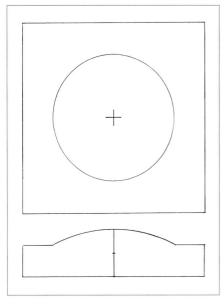

Hammer exercises – planishing. Radius is centred at 4¹/₄in.

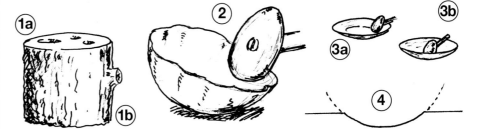

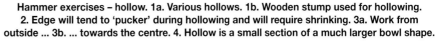

Hammer exercises – hollow. 1a. Various hollows. 1b. Wooden stump used for hollowing. 2. Edge will tend to 'pucker' during hollowing and will require shrinking. 3a. Work from outside ... 3b. ... towards the centre. 4. Hollow is a small section of a much larger bowl shape.

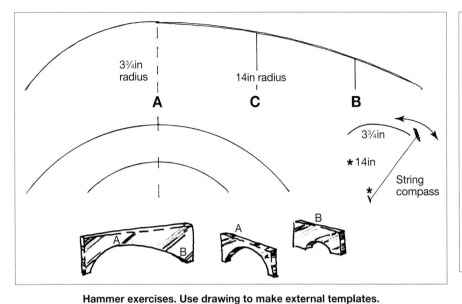

3¾in radius

14in radius

A **C** **B**

3¾in

★14in

★ 14in

String compass

Hammer exercises. Use drawing to make external templates.

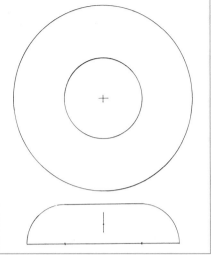

Hammer exercises – 6 inch bowl from 7 inch disk.

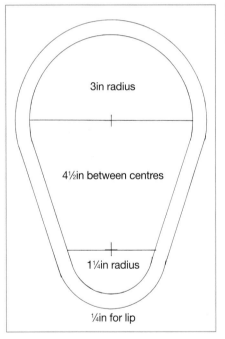

3in radius

4½in between centres

1¼in radius

¼in for lip

Hammer exercises – teardrop bowl.

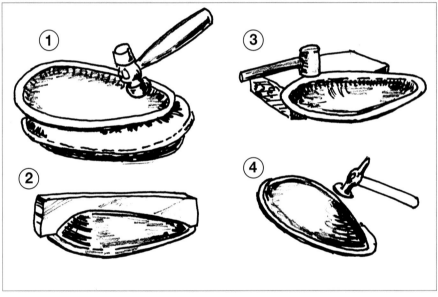

1. Stretch metal around periphery and work towards centre. 2. Check frequently with templates. 3. Dress flange. 4. Planish over dolly to finish.

Once the bowl is to shape, the entire surface can be planished lightly with overlapping blows which should impart a smooth surface. The finish can be perfected with draw filing and the use of wet and dry paper over a block. A mirror finish can then be attained with a little polishing.

6in bowl from a 7in disc!
This is a symmetrical bowl with a flat base. It is formed from a 7in disc, but finishes up as a 6in bowl. The circumference will need to be considerably reduced, the flat base will remain untouched, of course, and

the narrow band between these two areas will need to be stretched. If the exercise is completed correctly, the accompanying template should fit at any point.

Annealing
Annealing provides a way to break down or normalise the stresses built up in the metal during working. The process involves heating the metal until it starts to soften, though not so much as to make it collapse or melt. This is somewhat easier with steel than with aluminium, however, since steel glows red when it reaches the appropriate state, whereupon it can be left to cool. Aluminium, on the other hand, has a nasty habit of staying the same colour, and then

melting! A useful way to get around this problem in aluminium, is to first cover the areas to be annealed with carbon (using an oxyacetylene torch which has been set to burn an excess of acetylene). Then, with the torch set to a neutral flame, burn the carbon off. As well as removing the soot, this process will have provided enough heat to correctly anneal the aluminium. After five or ten minutes, the metal can be cooled off with water.

FOLDING, CURVING & SHRINKING
Bonnet (hood) scoop
Some years ago, a Stag I had worked on was found to be getting rather hot under

the collar. The combination of a bored-out Rover lump and a hot summer demanded that more air be passed over the plenum. My solution was a simple air scoop, and the range of processes employed in its production make it an excellent practice piece.

You can start by making sketches or by sticking folded bits or paper on your bonnet. Along with the overall positioning of the scoop, you'll need to decide on the length, width, and height of the scoop. Then you'll need to think about any crown on the top surface, how the opening is to be finished, and if the sides are to be angled. Finally, you'll need to consider the curve along the length which, I feel, should closely follow the original line of the bonnet. Make a card or plywood template of the bonnet curve, and use this to determine the final fit and the top curve (if you follow my design).

With all this information to hand, so to speak, you should be able to make a card mock-up for your design. The card can be persuaded to follow the curve by 'curfing' it to fit (cutting slits and bending a curve). You can also use the bonnet curve template to make a final template for the sides, which you can use to see how well the scoop will flow from the bonnet.

When the design is final, mark the dimensions on your sheet metal and add whatever return edges and mounting flanges are required. Do not mark fold lines with a scribe, though, as splitting may occur.

Having cut out the blank, the next step is to fold the sides over. I opted for a 70 degree bend, which I formed with my folder, though you might consider a softer radius on the edge.

The next step is to shrink the sides to gain the curve along the top. This can

be done by hand, as in the cold shrinking exercise outlined earlier, though a shrinking machine would make the job much easier. Work evenly along both sides and, when each follows the chosen line, smooth the sides to as good a finish as you can get.

Mark the bottom edge line (using your template), and dress it to form the flange which will mate with your bonnet. This process can be helped by 'jennying' the line, or forming the flange with a swager (beader). Jennying is the process of pinching the line between two fine wheels in order to break the surface tension and control the position of the bend line. I realise, of course, that few of you will have this equipment, but in an ideal world this equipment would be useful. Any movement of the sides caused while the flanges are being bent will need to be corrected. Positioning the scoop on the bonnet at this stage will give you a

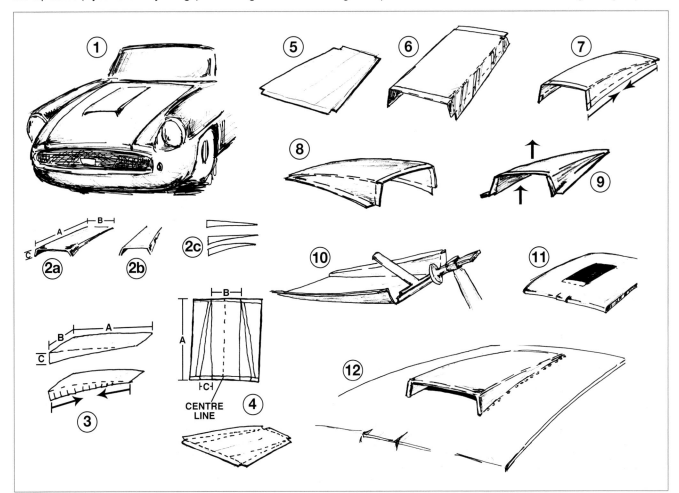

Hammer exercises. 1. We all have our own idea about what a bonnet scoop should look like. 2a. Decide first on the length, width and height ... 2b. ... the angle of sides, rise in top, crown etc. 2c. Consider profile. 3. A card mock-up will help with the final profile, or match to bonnet's line. 4. Mark-up and cut from fresh steel sheet. Include mounting flanges as required. 5. Metal blank. 6. Edges folded. A softer radius can be achieved by 'braking' over a T-stake. 7. Shrink sides – must be even. 8. Turn out mounting flanges with care. 9. Crown and mouth as required. 10. Fold or dress mouth over T-stake or bolster. 11. Hole in bonnet – allow for mountings. 12. Some filler is required at sides and rear to cover welds and seam.

good idea of how well it's going to fit and look.

It's unlikely that your bonnet is flat in any plane, so a flat top to your air intake may look a bit strange. I opted for a light crown through the mid-line, and a gentle curve to the opening.

To finish the job, you'll just need to tidy up the mouth. I'd recommend a gentle radius, rolled over a T-stake or bolster. Dress the edge carefully around the former, from the base of the curve. Split the corners, if necessary, so as to prevent any distortion. Once you've gained the desired effect, check and rectify any movement of the overall shape.

FABRICATION
Dorian's spoiler

Dorian Allery was a regular visitor to my little workshop for several years, before he finally entrusted me with the bodywork of his TVR-powered Stag. Dorian had often spoken of his wish for a bespoke front spoiler to replace the boxy appendage which housed his oversized radiator. This spoiler was to be smooth, subtle, and have lights built into it, and it had to direct air into engine bay. Although Dorian knew what he wanted, he was having trouble communicating the exact form to me, so, as the rebuild neared a end, I handed him my workshop keys, along with some card

and a roll of tape, and said "Make me half a spoiler."

Having tidied up Dorian's card mock-up to as close to the finished shape as was possible, the next step was to rationalise the design, by which I mean straightening the lines and marking a datum at the centre line. I also had to decide exactly where the new metal would join the old, how many pieces to use, how to shape each piece, and where these pieces would join. I could, of course, have made the thing in one piece, though that would have been difficult.

The final step, before any metal was bent, was to make a new, heavy card template (again, this only represented half of the design as the whole was symmetrical).

I fixed the flatish centre section in place while I finalised the lines of the two pieces that made up the corner. As you can see, the reverse curve would have been tricky to wrap around to the wing by beating alone. Twisting the bits into shape was pretty easy, and required only minor hammer work to tweak the top piece into mating exactly with the bottom.

The air slots and lamp holes were cut out with a hole punch and snips before being edge dressed to add a bit of rigidity and sharpen up the look.

The various pieces were then assembled, and the complete spoiler was attached to the car using a combination of spot welds, where access permitted, and MIG welds at the outside edges. The joints were then leaded and, for practicality, the valance was stone-chipped before the car was painted. Five years on it still looks great!

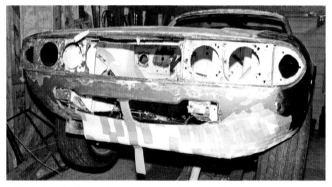

14-3a. Dorian's spoiler before ... an oversized rad sat in boxy add-on.

14-3b. Dorian's card and tape mock-up as I found it ... it's what I asked for!

14-3d. ... and sides. Practical and attractive.

14-3c. It's easier in sections. The centre ...

14-4. Rear of same car – I only put this in to show off.

Chapter 15
MGB face-lift

The styling of the original MGB was, to a great extent, inspired by the classic Aston DBs. The mid-1970s face-lift, however, was not so well received. Rubber bumper models don't realise the same prices as their chrome-bumpered siblings, and certainly don't turn heads in anything like the same way. I have long wanted to take a late MG, throw away that ugly bumper, and start again with a new front valance.

THE DESIGN
The initial problem is creating the design. Most people would insist that the station former (usually a template or model of the interior of the piece we are attempting to make), should be prepared from detailed drawings. However, in order to arrive at the draughting stage, I prefer to begin

15-1. This bumper is the result of US safety regs rather than aesthetics.

15-2. My original sketch.

by offering up bits of card to the car and marking out curves (and it's from these that I construct my drawings). You might also find it useful to doodle on photos or prints of the vehicle.

Constructing the station former
Unlike our previous formers, this one will be fabricated in plywood. Although its primary function is as a guide to the shape and curve of the new metal, it will also serve as a jig should you choose to make the panel in more than one piece. **Note!** The station former is not a beating buck or hammer form. At most, you may fix the metal to the buck for a bit of tweaking.

Stations run in the vertical plane fore and aft and laterally, with additional stations in the horizontal only if required. How you make them, and how many

stations you use will depend on your design. For our purposes, the fore to aft horizontal can be taken from the line of the sill, though we must also establish the centre line of the vehicle and our buck.

Creating the blank
The size and shape of the blank will be determined by the methods you're going to use to form your panel. If you only intend to wheel and planish the piece, for example, then you'll need a blank whose outline matches and follows the peripheral outline of the new piece. If you only intend to shrink your panel, start with a blank which measures the same as the new panel across its surface in all planes, and would therefore be larger around its periphery than the finished piece. In the real world, of course, you'd normally employ a combination of techniques, so your blank will, inevitably, be a compromise.

Placing a piece of strong paper over the former will help you determine the techniques you'll need to use. Mark the areas for shrinking and stretching *on the paper*, as well as any other information that might assist you later, and then cut out your blank (make it larger than you need, since it's easier to trim off excess metal than it is to add it).

Hollowing, raising & planishing
I usually begin a panel beating job by hollowing as I make faster progress that

15-3. Deciding on line of front curve.

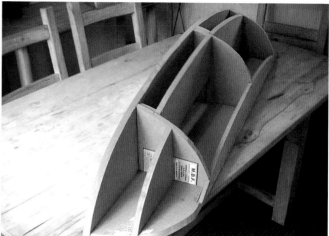

15-6. The station former.

15-4. Continue line from side of wing ...

15-7. Panel must be checked against buck at all stages of formation.

15-5. ... and a line to work to.

15-8. Paper template is formed over buck.

way. In this case, because I was using steel (and because I wanted to stretch as well as shape), I began with a heavy ball-pien. I then continued the process with a heavy hide mallet, which softened

the effect of the steel hammer and finally used a combination of hide, urethane and boxwood mallets for some raising over my standard dollies.

Frequent checking of the station

former kept me true to the original design, and showed me where I needed to concentrate my efforts. (Incidentally, I find it is easiest to do the shrinking over the dolly using a bumping hammer for the

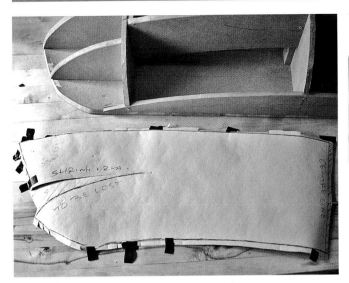

15-9. Paper helps to rationalise the metalwork.

15-12. Additional section.

15-10. Blank ready for working.

15-13. Panel takes shape.

15-11. Planishing over a dolly.

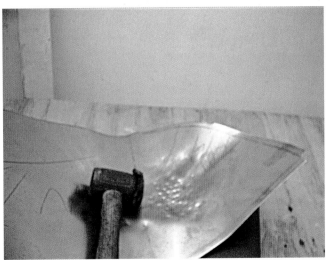

15-14. Early mallet work.

15-15. Spot the similarity.

15-16. The finished piece with the station former is the result of three template curves.

It's up to you when you cut out the air slots, etc, though it's probably easier to do so before the panel is attached to the car.

Edge treatments fall into two categories: applied (where the edge stiffening is made up separately and then fixed to the panel); and formed (where the edge stiffening is formed from the metal of the panel itself).

Folding

Folding is edge finishing in its simplest form. The fold may be single, double or stepped. Take a look at any older vehicle to see the huge range and variation of applications for this essentially simple process.

Flanging

This technique simply involves turning the metal at right angles to the panel, as in a wheelarch, for example. The flange can be further strengthened and

protected, however, by the application of a cap. The disadvantage of this method of edge finishing is that any blow to the edge will result in stretching, and possible fracture of the flange, which will prove very resistant to repair. Panels joined with a flange will require great care when the flange is being formed so as not to throw out of whack the line of the panel. Traditionally this sort of flange is produced by passing the edge of the panel through a swager set with the appropriate wheels: however it is not uncommon for at least some of the flange to be produced entirely by hand.

Swaging

The swager is also used to impart shape and add rigidity to panel edges. The swager can also be used to produce joddled edges which are used in creased lap joints.

Wire-wound edging

Wire-wound edging is a traditional edge treatment that has remained popular with the world's military, along with manufacturers of agricultural machinery and heavy goods vehicles. Wire-wound edges are very resilient and hard wearing, but rather difficult to repair as the metal tends to stretch and split at the point of impact. The nature of the edging also makes it a perfect water trap.

Wire-wound edges can take one of three forms depending on where the wire sits relative to the panel edge. You will find some configurations easier than others to replicate or repair.

Traditionally, the wire can be set by hand or using a swager fitted with wiring rolls. The swager will give a neater final finish, but usually demands a second pair of hands.

tuck and a boxwood mallet for the actual shrinking blows.)

When completely happy with the shape, I planished the entire surface using a light bumping hammer over a heel dolly. The aim in planishing, of course, was to produce a uniform finish rather than add any more shape.

Remember that, when raising and planishing, the metal is worked from the centre outwards, and when hollowing, from the outer regions inward.

FINISHING THE EDGES

Once the piece has been shaped, the next step is to tidy the edges and/or produce the flanges required for fixing the panel to the vehicle. Care must be taken not to undo any earlier work as, once the edges are set, the piece will no longer fit the former, and the edges will also offer resistance to further forming.

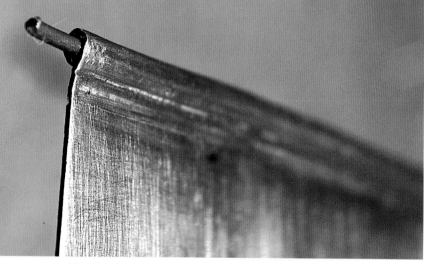

15-17. Wire-wound edge using 2mm copper-coated wire.

15-18. Swager rolls used to close wire-wound edges.

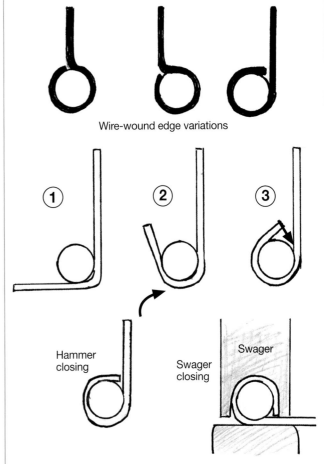

Wire-wound edge variations

15-19. Wire-wound process.

Whichever method you find works for you, you will undoubtedly find that a clear flat beating block on a bench will aid progress no end. Some sheet-metal rollers will also feature wire mills that can be used for the job.

To create a wire-wound edge:
1. Form a right-angled flange around the periphery of the panel with a depth equal to the circumference of your chosen wire. You will find that to form this flange around a wheelarch will demand some stretching and shrinking of the metal, which may lead to brittleness at the next stage of the process. Consider annealing, but be wary of the possibility of distortion to flat areas. A soft radius that matches the wire will usually be preferable to a sharp fold. So if using a box-folder or metal-brake, you could form the bend in two stages. If forming it by hammer, consider the use of an appropriate T-stake.

Please note that for an external or opposite wire the flange must be turned outward, while the internal wire requires the flange to be turned inward.
2. Start at one end of the panel and set the wire into place with an appropriate clamp. Whether or not you chose to form the wire into shape (to match the periphery) prior to insertion is up to you – it may be easier to tweak it to fit as you go along.
3. Turn the flange over the wire in stages to avoid puckering or further stretching

of the metal. Be sure to move clamps as you go (to keep them from obstructing the turned edge) in such a way that they hold the wire hard into the edge as you work along the panel.

The initial stages of turning the edge over can be performed with a mallet or bumping hammer. A urethane mallet will give good movement without undue stretching, but the choice of hammer is up to the individual.
4. Finish by tucking the edge over the wire to close it. This is best done with a cross-pein hammer or with the wiring rolls on a swager. A chase wedge or bolster might also be used for the final tucking in.

Welding panel sections
If your panel is being fabricated from more than one piece, it's very important that you consider the position of the joins, especially with regard to heat dissipation, access to the weld area, and location with regard to the former. It's quite acceptable to fix any and all sections of your panel onto the former (using nails or screws), but make sure you fill all holes with weld.

Carefully align the sections so that

very close fitting butt joints can be used (without additional filler material which might lead to problems when you come to planishing). Once aligned, the sections should be tack welded together (at intervals of about 1 inch/25mm) and each tack should be allowed to cool before you proceed to the next one, thus ensuring minimal distortion and reducing the risk of damage to your wooden former. As the face of your work is to be machined, it's imperative that your weld has adequate penetration, though not so much as to leave a surplus. Generally, it's thought best to weld small sections at a time which are then dressed to shape while hot, as this adds strength and reduces the amount of grinding required. If carried out correctly, your joint should be almost invisible.

Thanks to Batemans Performance and Restoration in Ashington for helping with some of the pictures in this chapter.

Chapter 16
Panel repair techniques

PRINCIPLES

The principles of panel formation, and many of the techniques involved, are also applicable to panel repair. Before we can look at panel repair in a systematic way, though, we must first understand something of the characteristics of sheet metal in the context of vehicle production.

When sheet metal is bent into a soft arc and then released, it will usually spring back to its former shape. If the same sheet is bent past its limit of elasticity, however, some of the new shape will be retained due to stresses imparted to the newly-formed curve. If we consider the sheet in its original state to be of uniform thickness and density, then we must now consider the outer portion of the bent area to have stretched and the inner portion to have contracted. These stresses will cause the metal to work harden and, in extreme cases, become brittle. Body panels which have been pressed will also have had stresses imparted to them, and these, along with any additional stresses caused by impact, must be considered carefully if we are not to waste many hours attempting to repair accident damage.

It should also be remembered that, during pressing, the outer surface of a panel, even in low-crowned areas, will have been affected by the press dies, and will be work hardened in much the same way as ordinary sheet steel which has been rolled to impart a surface tension.

ASSESSMENT

Any panel can be thought of as consisting of a combination of rigid or elastic (high- and low-crowned) areas. As well as the more obvious double curved applications, the term high-crown also refers to swages and ridges.

Damage rectification can be divided into two stages: roughing out, during which the reinforced sections are straightened and the panel is returned to its approximate shape; and finishing, during which the surface is returned to a smooth state by means of hammer and dolly, bumping file and body file.

It's often tempting to apply brute force to the lowest areas of damage in the belief that this will bring the panel back into shape. However, this will may stretch previously undamaged metal and won't relieve the abnormal stresses which are actually holding the panel out of shape. The best way to undo the damage is by lifting the dent from the lowest point in a way that won't stretch the metal, while at the same time relieving the stresses in the surrounding and corresponding high points and creases.

ROUGHING OUT

Roughing out is the process of knocking a panel back into some semblance of its prior shape. Although this can mean using a sledge hammer or a hydraulic puller, for the purposes of this book, though, I think we should limit ourselves to localised

panel repairs with a heavy mallet, hammer or dolly. Bear in mind that it's the tight areas, such as creases, which hold the tension and prevent your panel from returning to its former shape.

Most roughing out techniques are carried out from the inside of the damaged panel, so the task is often hampered by lack of clearance and visibility. When roughing out with a dolly, choose a profile that won't unduly mar the panel, and aim for the centre of the dent. You'll get better accuracy if you hold a finger on the outside of the panel in the appropriate spot.

A light blow from a heavy hammer will produce the most movement, so it's a good idea to place a wooden or rubber block between the hammer and the panel to dissipate the blow. This is the principle behind the use of the spring hammer, which is held flat against a high point or ridge and then struck with a heavy hammer. If the panel is held in tension, the effect is amplified. This technique is also employed to reduce high points after planishing as it can have the effect of shrinking the excess metal back into itself.

HAMMER & DOLLY WORK

If you've followed the exercises in the previous sections you'll know that, in panel beating, the hammer is employed in a very different fashion to most other disciplines. In general, the hammer is held loosely, and is allowed to rebound naturally. There is no follow through, and no attempt to punch the work as you would a nail. Failure to hold the hammer in this manner will soon result in fatigue or injury. You'll also find this method improves accuracy, which is of considerable concern.

Ideally, your dolly should weigh approximately three times that of the hammer, and you should stand in a slightly bent-kneed 'fighting' stance with one foot forward under the dolly hand. Allow the dolly to rest loosely in the lower hand so that only its weight is used rather than exerting a lifting pressure. The hammer should also be held in a loose fist. Practice rhythmically tapping the hammer onto the dolly to produce a 'ringing' which signifies that the dolly is being struck squarely. The dolly should be allowed to rebound slightly, but not so much as to produce a double-blow.

For panel repairs, hammers and dollies can be used in two ways:

Indirect hammering
In this technique, the hammer is brought down on the metal slightly to one side of the dolly, and makes use of the dolly's rebound effect. This method is most useful in situations where metal which has not received a lot of damage can be persuaded to return to its original form. When lifting a dent, it may be possible to apply a lifting pressure to the lowest point while tapping around the corresponding high.

Indirect hammering is also employed to great effect when gathering up slack (see the section on hot-shrinking).

Direct hammering
Direct hammering is basically planishing, though in this instance, it's used to refinish rather than finish. The process is the same, but the application different. Before you can begin planishing it's imperative to clean the underside of your panel (mud and underseal will absorb your hammer blow and impart an uneven surface to your work and dolly). The dolly must also be carefully selected as too high a crown would result in an unwanted fullness (or high) to the repair. Too low a crown and the repair would tend to flatten out. It's a good idea to start beating with a few light (and ineffective) blows, as these will ensure that the dolly is being hit squarely. Failure to correctly strike over your dolly will result in the opposite of the desired effect.

The area of impact during planishing is very small, even when using a broad-faced bumping hammer and large dolly. The rest of the dolly/hammer profile can be thought of as having a supporting roll.

Whichever technique you employ, the aim is always to lift the area of metal directly over the dolly. As the job progresses, you may need to use a body file or similar device in order to see where the lows and highs are (see the section on metal finishing).

OTHER PANEL BEATING TECHNIQUES
Spring hammering
It's possible to dress high points from the outside using a spring hammer (held flat over the panel and beaten with a hammer). This method relies on the strength of the crown to support the surface being worked without the use of a dolly. The spring hammer can also be used in a slapping fashion, or to beat directly onto the metal. Always begin with light blows, though, as it's possible to dress the metal too far resulting in a low or flat. Spring hammers can be either flat or crowned and are easily made from old cart springs.

Pick hammer
Picking up a dent is a risky technique in the hands of the novice. The idea is to lift the dent with series of well placed blows from the pick hammer, the pimples or high points which result are then dressed by planishing to level the panel. Injudicious use of the pick will result in stretching and further damage.

Hot-shrinking
This is one of the key techniques in damage repair. The principle is simply that, during an impact, unwanted stretching often occurs and, in order to return the panel to its pre-accident condition, we have to lose the excess surface area. The process involves gathering up the slack, heating it red, and driving it back into itself. This is a highly-skilled operation, with a lot of scope for things to go wrong.

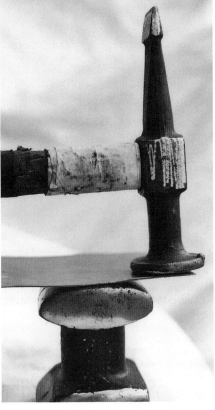

16-1. Beating off the dolly.

16-2. Beating on the dolly.

16-3. Use of the spring hammer.

For hot-shrinking, you'll need the following equipment/materials: oxyacetylene gear with a stand for the torch (no. 2 nozzle or smaller); a boxwood mallet, planishing or grid-faced shrinking hammer, and a dolly of the correct profile, plus a round dolly for gathering up the slack; a damp cloth and water for quenching and to control distortion; Cold-front ceramic paste (this is optional, but jolly useful for limiting heat damage); a wire brush, scraper, etc, to remove paint and underseal; all relevant safety gear.

You might be shocked to learn that metal actually shrinks after being heated. Although it expands when first heated, when metal cools it contracts beyond its original form. If we apply localised heat to a crowned area, for example, it will initially rise, but then fall back to a lower position when it cools. This is very handy for those of us with stretched panels.

Gather up the slack with a round dolly and either a boxwood mallet or a bumping hammer. Think of the metal as if it were a fluid, and move the 'wave' of

slack to where you want it, by pushing up with the dolly and lightly dressing around it. A peak of excess metal can be formed, leaving the surrounding panel in its correct profile.

Heat a spot in the centre of the raised metal to a bright cherry red by aiming the torch squarely at the centre of the boss and then circling it before returning the flame to the centre. The centre will rise further than the surrounding area. Place the torch on its stand and, using the boxwood

16-6. Circle with flame ...

16-7. ... and pull flame into centre.

16-4 to 16-17. Sequence shows hot-shrinking.

16-4. Hammer and dolly used to gather slack prior to shrinking.

16-8. Use mallet around periphery ...

16-5. A lump suitable for shrinking – in fact, I formed this with a heavy hammer.

16-9. ... before knocking down centre.

16-10. Work fast.

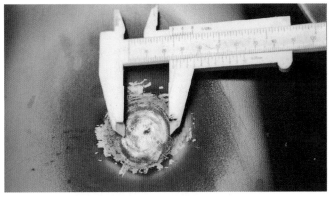

16-11. Maximum size to be heated or risk distortion.

16-12. Beating off the dolly will raise low centre.

16-13. Beating on the dolly will also raise low centre.

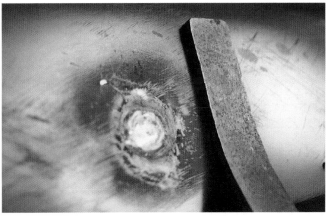

16-14. Use of the bumping file: it will contact a larger area.

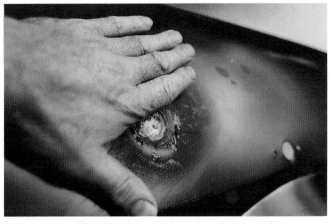

16-15. There is no substitute for hands.

16-16. Bumping file leaves knurling marks, while body file removes them.

mallet, smack the high point straight back into itself. An alternative would be to strike a ring of blows around the centre of the hot spot, thus driving the surplus metal into the centre. Follow these up with a final blow directly onto the centre of the spot.

Whichever method you opt for, hold the dolly loosely under the heated area and take care not to stretch the metal further (metal hammers will also tend to stretch the metal and are not advised for the beginner). Quench the panel immediately after malleting so as to stop the spread

16-17. Use of body file.

of the heat. The operation can now be repeated as necessary.

Note!
• Never heat an area bigger than you can shrink. 10mm will do for starters; the maximum is 25mm.
• Only use oxyacetylene for shrinking, as too soft a flame will heat too large an area.
• Never quench a red-hot area; black is safer.
• One well-placed shrink is always desirable.
• In the case of multiple heat spots, drawing out the heat expansion with quenching will reduce the number of shrinks required.
• Some prefer to use a grid-faced shrinking hammer for this job.
• When heat shrinking aluminium, it's necessary to work very quickly, as this material is a particularly good heat conductor. Bear in mind that aluminium will not glow red, as steel does, but will tend to melt! Try giving it a coating of soot from a reduced flame and then burn it off with a neutral flame; that should bring the area up to temperature.
• After shrinking, the repair area will require planishing.

Faux shrinking
This is a cold shrinking method which only appears to shrink the panel, though you may encounter circumstances when this will have to do.

The shrinking dolly is a flat dolly with a deep groove running down the centre of its crowned face. By gathering up the slack and working it into the groove with a cross pien, a stretched panel can be restored to its proper contour. The slack is then filled in with lead (traditionally) or polyester filler.

METAL FINISHING
Traditionally, the aim with every repair was the 'metal finish,' i.e. a repair without filler. In the modern bodyshop, however, this ideal is all but lost. Pressure of time and modern techniques have seen an end to the fillerless repair. Newer vehicles and alloys do not lend themselves to metal finishing, and the time needed to perfect the art is no longer invested in training. This is a shame really because, in many cases, the metal finish need take no longer.

The body file
The flexible body file is used to perfect the metal finish. It consists of a very hard steel file blade with serrations milled into it in such a way as to prevent clogging. The file holder has two handles, and a turnbuckle which allows the blade to be bent concave or convex in order to follow the curvature of the panel. Wooden-handled, straight body files are also available, and can be either flat or round faced.

The aim of the body file is to reveal the highs and lows and impart a smooth finish rather than remove lots of metal.

The bumping file
The bumping file, when used in conjunction with a dolly and body file, will raise low points as they are revealed without undue stretching. It will impart a knurled finish which aids the revelation, and which can be removed easily by subsequent use of the body file. The bumping file, whether used with a dolly for lifting a low, or without for dressing down a high, will utilise the support of the surrounding metal, and with a bit of care will do no damage other than to impart knurling.

FINISHING UP
Having brought the panel up to shape by planishing, check the contour by passing the flexible body file over the repair. The body file should be applied with long straight strokes, rather than jabs, though the exact direction of the file stroke is governed by the contour of the panel. Generally speaking, you'll have to hold the file in such as way as to contact as much metal as possible. If you do it right, the low points will reveal themselves as areas with no file marks. If only a few points contact the file, then these can be considered highs, and the panel dressed accordingly.

As the job progresses, you should use only the bumping file and suitable dolly. Between dressings, repeat the filing process in as many planes and directions as you can, as working in one direction will only reveal some of the shape. Gradually, more of the repair should show file marks as the panel returns to its true shape. Repeatedly filing high peaks increases the risk of filing through, so only light pressure should be employed when filing.

Obviously, this technique is limited to repairs where access permits.

A compromise between a pure metal finish and pressure to get the job done, is to use the same techniques but skim the final few millimetres with filler, and file in the usual manner.

Chapter 17
Bracing & structural support

BODY BRACING & DIMENSIONAL INTEGRITY

It is all too easy when carrying out restoration work to allow some sections of the car to move relative to others, thus resulting in doors that do not quite align or worse, do not close. In more serious cases, body shells have been rendered dangerous to drive or fit only for scrap.

Often it is merely a lack of forethought, excessive zeal, or simply an uneven floor which has led to the problem. Other times, inexperience and a lack of advice will lead the restorer out of his depth. A job which begins as a simple wing replacement may well end up with a sill being removed.

Either way, it obviously pays to speak to people who have previously done the particular job to appreciate what problems you may face. For example, anyone who has ever replaced the sills on a Midget will tell you that the door gaps can move, even if you put a brace across the aperture. And anyone who has ever restored a Jaguar saloon will tell you that they are heavy, complicated structures, requiring a lot of support if you are planning on removing any of the important sections.

And it goes without saying that it takes a lot more force to straighten a Jaguar shell than it does to realign something like a Midget. Far better to get it right than to rectify; which may involve unpicking, cutting or sacrificing previous work, and even the destruction of newly fitted panels.

So what do we do?

Forewarned is forearmed and a belt and braces approach will usually hold you in good stead. Take a good look around your car before you undo anything. Take pictures of panel gaps and door lines. It is possible to get hung up on perfection at the end of the process, when your car had never been that way when it left the factory. My mentor, Mr Smith, always told how, while working at a BL main dealership, customers would point out mismatched gaps on cars which had been repaired. Smithy would hand them a vernier gauge and quietly lead them into the showroom. Here, the brand new Heralds would prove just how random the gaps could be. Our current trend for perfect gaps belies the truth of many of our domestic classics.

AND IF YOU ARE UNSURE OF YOUR CAR'S STRAIGHTNESS?

If the panels on your car do not line up and you suspect the chassis to be out of line, you would do well to take it to a body shop where the car can be placed on a jig for measurement and correction. Before you do this, though, it might be a good idea to carry out a simple drop check.

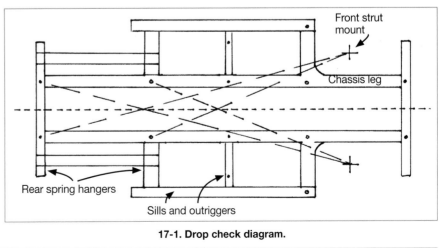

17-1. Drop check diagram.

The simple drop check

The drop check is the easiest way to check a vehicle's alignment and requires only a plum bob, some chalk and a smooth, level floor. The idea is to use pairs of symmetrical points from the rear of the chassis and link them to pairs of symmetrical points at the front diagonally across a centre line. If the pairs do not converge along the centre line, then the car is not symmetrical along its centre line – possibly due to some foreshortening caused by impact.

To perform the check:

Set the car level on stands (level is taken to be with the sills parallel to the floor). Now start at the rear of the car, assuming the problem is at the front. Use the plum bob to mark the floor on line with as many paired fixed points on the chassis as you can find. Work your way forward, continuing to mark points on the floor.

It was common practice to mark a large target area with the chalk and then use a pencil or crayon to mark the exact point. Take care not to crawl over previous markings.

When the initial marking is complete, it will help if you can remove the car, but in practice, this is not always so easy.

Now decide which pairs of rear marks should be mated to which others; remember that any misalignment needs to be interpreted, so it pays to work from front to back with this in mind. Pairs from the rear can be linked to pairs from the middle of the car, before being linked to pairs at the front. In this way, the rear half of the chassis can (hopefully) be seen as correct, before a problem at the front shows up.

A string can be used to link diagonal pairs of marks and the point at which they cross the centre can be marked with chalk or crayon if a long straight edge is not available.

Traditionally, a tolerance of +/- ⅛in was considered acceptable.

The hanging parallel check

Another common, simple, low-tech check was to use wire hooks to suspend straight bars (rulers, broom handles etc) below the chassis from pairs of symmetrical points on either side. If the wires are of equal length, the bars should all be parallel when viewed from the front of the vehicle. If not, the discrepancy may be due to impact damage that has caused a section to lift or drop. You will also see how the bumper, grille, lights, bonnet edge and scuttle fit into this pattern. It is important when carrying out checks of this type that an uneven floor not be allowed to throw the eye.

SETTING UP A CAR FOR STRUCTURAL WORK

The degree of support your particular car will require will depend on several factors. Some models from the seventies in particular were not known for being very rigid, even when new. The local Constabulary used to drive around in Austin Allegro's, which wore stickers on the sills reading 'Do not lift this vehicle using this jacking point' because the bodyshell would distort so much that the doors would no longer open or close. Likewise, the Triumph Stag is well known for not holding its shape if supported other than by its wheels.

17-2. A plum-bob can be hung from pairs of location points. Use chalk to highlight the area and pen/pencil to pin-point the position, as the workshop floor may conceal detail.

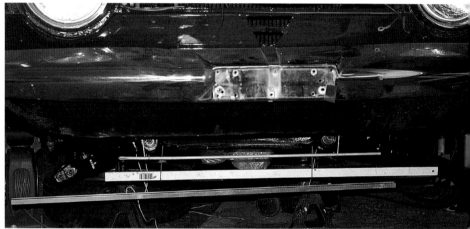

17-3. Hanging parallel using welding wire hooks and random straight pieces.

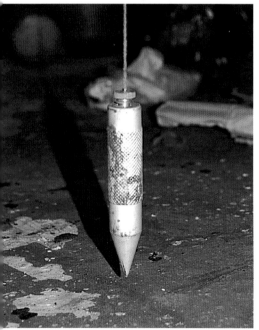

17-4. Pairs of wire hooks must be equally-sized and hung to give usable results.

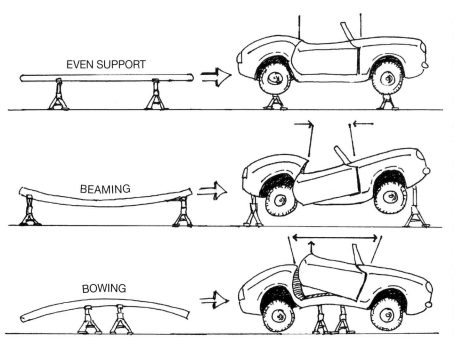

EVEN SUPPORT

BEAMING

BOWING

17-5. Even support, beaming and bowing diagram.

under the car, but have certain drawbacks for general bodywork. The flat folding ramp, as used in the section featuring Dorian's spoiler (page 104), is an elegant solution to most of our lifting problems.

Body rollers are advertised as a means of working on the underside of a vehicle. Typically, the bodyshell is mounted on the roller by the bumper mounts, which are usually at the ends of the chassis rails. I would have to advise extreme caution when considering the use of these devices, as they rely entirely on the ability of the chassis rails to support the cars weight without beaming or bowing. Given that many vehicles are designed with the roof acting as a compression member, don't be surprised if it cannot fulfil this role if the structure is inverted. Likewise, the removal of any critical member might mean serious damage. Also, many of our cars do not actually have any chassis beyond the rear axle, so the bumpers are effectively mounted onto a big hollow box, which is the boot. Other models have chassis rails that run only to an area below the seats where the load is transferred to the sills via out riggers.

When working on a Stag, I will keep it on its wheels as much as possible, and only check panel alignment when the car is squarely on the floor.

Most other vehicles can be safely set at a comfortable working height on axle stands, but it is always worth making it level, if your floor is not, especially if there is any risk that your working will compromise the structural integrity (ie sill removal).

In most cases, two pairs of axle stands will suffice, but it never hurts to add more support as the job progresses. A block or scissor jack under the dash/scuttle is a good idea if the A-post is to be disturbed. An extra set of axle stands under the chassis midway along the car is a must if both the chassis rails and sills are being cut.

Again, forethought is key. Look at the car, where is the weight? How will it move if one or other member is cut or removed? Trestles and wooden beams can be put to good use. You cannot have too much support.

Ramps, lifts & body-rollers
Standard ramps are an easy way of gaining height for working under the car, but don't usually give a huge amount of lift. One pair of ramps used in conjunction with a trolley jack and a pair of axle stands will do for a variety of jobs. Large ramps (as shown in the accompanying photos) require a large area of level floor, but ensure good lift and a stable platform.

Two and four post hydraulic lifts, as used in garages, are lovely for working

17-6-17-9. Supporting an MGB on ramps.

17-6. These giant ramps require a lot of space.

17-7. Gently does it ...

17-8. Jack used to raise the rear of the car.

17-9. Legs can now be used to secure the ramps level for safe working.

BRACING
Door aperture braces

The simplest form of body bracing is the proprietary door brace, which can be found in a lot of restoration supply outlets. Expanding door aperture braces have the added advantage that they can be used to effect some movement of the aperture, either to push or pull whilst clamped into the frame. They also remain solid in both compression and tension. This type of brace is adjustable between 830mm and 1160mm, making them suitable for many of our cars, but by no means all of them. You cannot use these braces for many of the smaller British models, including the Midget/Sprite family and often the Spitfire/GT6.

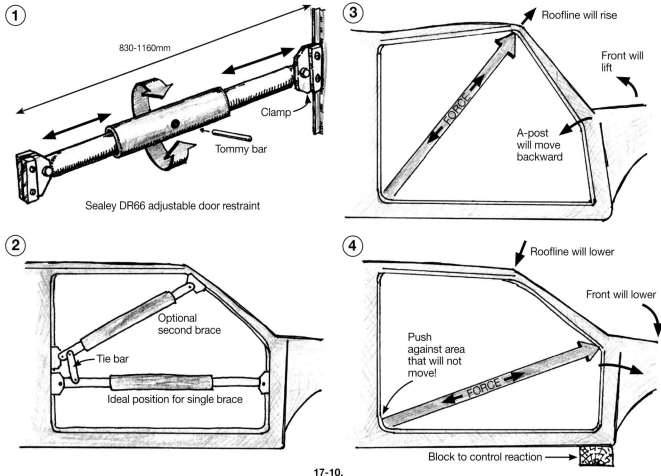

① 830-1160mm

Clamp

Tommy bar

Sealey DR66 adjustable door restraint

② Optional second brace

Tie bar

Ideal position for single brace

③ Roofline will rise

FORCE

Front will lift

A-post will move backward

④ Roofline will lower

Front will lower

Push against area that will not move!

FORCE

Block to control reaction

17-10.

If you are able to employ this type of brace, it is usually well worth investing in a pair. In use, the braces can be fitted singularly or doubled up across one aperture or with one on each side of the car. Removal and refitting of the door should still be possible with the braces set in place.

DIY aperture braces
A cheaper and more customised solution is to fabricate your own bespoke braces, as shown in the Jaguar photos (right). The exact construction will be governed by your precise needs.

Whatever method you opt for, never trust the brace blindly. Always check the panel fit by eye at every stage of the process and especially before welding. With a particularly tricky customer like the Midget, I would tend to weld the brace across the aperture rather than trust a bolt – a less elegant solution, but ultimately, one which is more trustworthy.

Internal bracing
This is an area which is going to need your considered judgment with regard to when and where to place the bracing and how much is needed. It may be that you will be able to bolt the bars in place, but more likely you will have to tack straps across the shell.

Don't wait until the car has collapsed (as with the Jaguar shown), but rather anticipate the problems and get in there first.

Again, forethought is key. Where is the structure going move if any particular part is removed or cut? Where can the brace work best in tension? Will the anchor point move?

5mm mild steel bar is readily available and can be cut and bent to suit any situation. Its main strength is tensile, so use it to hold against the direction of where the car might elongate. Bracing across the car (as shown between the b-post) is mainly to help locate the new sill.

Bear in mind that you may have to get into the car to work, and that the bracing will have to be removed without further damage. At the rear of the car I set a bar through the rear window aperture toward the boot floor. This precluded a trial fit of the boot lid, which at the time was obviously a lesser priority.

17-10 Left: Door brace and pushing across door aperture diagrams: 1. Proprietary door aperture retainers can be used to push and pull. 2. Ideal position of braces, either singular or in pairs. 3. Force directed to top front of aperture will cause the front of the car to lift. 4. Force to middle of aperture will cause the front of the car to lower.

17-11-17-16. Jaguar shell being pushed and braced.

17-11. Driver's door gap indicates more pushing is required.

17-12. Only when doors align should bracework be fitted in place for welding.

17-13. Bracing complete across one side allows for door closure.

Rectification & bracing

My involvement with the Jaguar shell began only after the structure had moved. So the first job was to set the thing right before any bracing could be installed.

The key here was assessing, understanding and measuring the problem. Do not be tempted to jump in with the push-rams and hope for the best.

The doors will provide the biggest clue as to what is wrong, and a 'panel fit diagram' will clarify what has moved where, which in turn will help you put it all back where it should be. Less obvious, but equally important, are considerations concerning what has recently been done to the car, and how it has been handled. A look underneath the Jaguar showed a general lack of support, but further investigation revealed that the bodyshell had been lifted across too narrow a section of the chassis (typical of pallet or fork-lift), and had at some point suffered a kink to the chassis rail almost in line with the driver's A-post. The collapse had occurred only when the outrigger/jacking-point that bridges between the chassis rail and the sill/A-post was removed. When complete, the Jaguar shell, though heavy, is in fact very rigid. But in this case, a number of factors had conspired to create what was really a very serious failure. The mis-register between the front doors and the B-post was so great that a fist could be passed into the gap at the top rear corner.

A Porto-power hydraulic ram set is common to most body shops, and comes with a variety of extension tubes and ends which allow the pressure to be applied exactly where it is wanted. This equipment is capable of doing a lot of damage, so if you have any doubts about using it, DON'T.

Working on the Jaguar, the ram was used to push between the lower rear and top front corners of the front door aperture. This had the effect of lifting the front of the car. Had we pushed into the middle of the front (bottom of the screen pillar), the effect would have been to lower the front, and thus make things worse. A push to the area between the top front and mid front would have buckled the screen pillars irreversibly.

SAFETY

All of the procedures detailed in this chapter involve some risk to your vehicle and, indeed, yourself. The responsibility for safety and the dimensions of your car is very much your own.

Having set your car securely on stands, it is wise to give it a 'shove' before placing yourself underneath it – if it is going to fall, don't have it fall on you!

17-14. Porto-power hydraulic ram in situ. Care must be taken to prevent damage to flanges.

17-15. Driver's door with frame fitted confirms correct angle of A-post.

17-16. Rear of NSF door shows even gap and reasonable swage alignment.

Chapter 18
Guide to welding

WHICH METHOD?

Bodywork restoration is all about light gauge steel sheet and your ability to weld it. But which method (or methods) of welding should you opt for?

In the mid-eighties the MIG welder revolutionised welding by offering a simple and quick method that pretty much anyone could learn. Prior to this, it was oxyacetylene gas welding that ruled the body shop. Within the vehicle construction industry, the resistance spot welder has been the norm since the '30s, though for various reasons, has never caught on with the domestic market. Arc welding (stick-welding, MMA) has been around for many years, but other than in the hands of a very experienced and skilled man, is too coarse for use on the 20 and 18swg we are concerned with.

Today, the TIG welder has surfaced as a new contender, when only a few years ago, this method was considered too costly and too tricky for the likes of us.

18-1. The MIG welder lends itself well to car repair and restoration.

OXYACETYLENE GAS WELDING

Gas welding has long since been regarded as the authentic method for the craftsman, and for that reason alone, will always have a following. In the right hands, gas welding is a truly elegant craft, but is not without its drawbacks, some of which are serious and potentially very dangerous. Gas welding is reliant on compressed gasses stored in heavy bottles and transmitted through rubber hoses via brass valves and fittings. The equipment is cumbersome, and in use, the torch produces a flame which is in excess of a thousand degrees at one point, but invisible for many inches beyond.

The principal of gas welding is to heat two pieces of metal until they fuse to become one. Additional material is added where necessary by means of a filler rod, which is fed manually into the weld pool.

Gas welding is a relatively slow process and needs a fair bit of practise before any real work can be undertaken. Even with experience, gas welding inevitably results in a lot of residual heat being transmitted into the panel, and the constant risk of the flame playing over areas where it is not welcome. Procedures such as hammer-welding, which demand that the torch be set down quickly while you work the hot metal, pose a temptation to not turn it off, the consequences of which could be catastrophic.

Gas brazing is similar to gas welding and poses many of the same risks, and problems. Where with true welding the

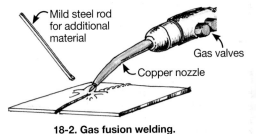

18-2. Gas fusion welding.

Mild steel rod for additional material

Gas valves

Copper nozzle

Brass rod

Brass rod

Brazing

Brass welding

18-3. Gas brazing and gas brass welding.

aim is to fuse two pieces of metal, brazing involves using alloy, which melts at a lower temperature to flow by capillary attraction between the pieces and bond to both. Though the joint is not as strong as true welding, it covers a larger surface area and produces similar results in real terms. Brazing uses a 'softer' flame than welding. This flame, though not as hot, can in fact contain more heat. Brazing is not considered a proper repair or joining method for structural members in the eyes of the MoT inspectorate.

Brass/bronze welding differs from brazing in that, instead of employing capillary attraction to run the alloy between the pieces, a shoulder of alloy is built up at the point of joining. This method produces a hugely strong joint and is still favoured by traditional specialists for fabricating motorcycle frames.

Braze (brass) and bronze are differentiated by their respective copper content. Bronze requires more heat and is generally harder and forms a stronger bond. As a confusing aside, the term 'brazing' can refer to the brazier or hearth, and so may not involve any brass. Silver solder (hard-solder) has a melting point in excess of 400 degrees and should more correctly be called silver-brazing. Silver-soldering can be used in bodywork and is capable of joining some dissimilar metals.

Cost & equipment

A full-sized gas welding set will set you back about £200. On top of this you

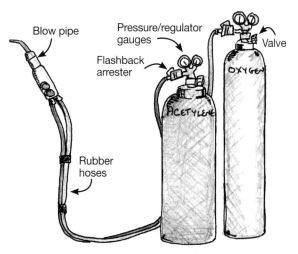

18-4. Drawing of gas welding gear.

18-5. Portapack gas welding gear.

will have to rent gas bottles and pay for them to be filled as required. All told, the initial outlay is likely to be in the region of £300-350, plus there will be a yearly rental commitment regardless of how much gas you actually consume.

As an alternative, you may opt for the popular 'Turbo-gas' set, which is available from Weld UK at around £120. It comes complete with a range of gas nozzles and is ideal for the small-scale consumer. However, the miniature gas bottles have a limited run-time and the economy is skewed if more than a small amount of welding is required. In particular, learning to weld using this equipment may prove costly. You would be well advised to order two bottles of oxygen for every bottle of fuel. Other mini welding sets are available. The Turbo-gas system uses Mapp gas LPG as a fuel, which burns hotter than Propane, commonly used in blow torches and some mini weld/braze sets.

Safety considerations of gas welding

Oxygen is not actually flammable, but it will actively encourage any combustible material to burn readily. Oxygen in full-sized bottles is supplied at a pressure of 3000psi, which, without any flame, is enough to do serious damage to person or property.

Acetylene is a highly explosive gas unstable at any pressure above two atmospheres (30psi). It is supplied at a pressure of 240psi; dissolved in acetone and held in a mixture of charcoal and concrete within a steel bottle.

Full gas handling and safety instruction will be supplied by BOC, which must

18-6. Full-sized gas welding set with in-line fluxer.

be read and fully complied with. In the event of a workshop fire you may be required to move the bottles to a place of safety. You should also consider the proximity of other buildings and people before introducing gas bottles of any kind into your workplace.

All fumes created by welding should be regarded as hazardous. Brazing will demand the use of a flux, which is probably acidic, and any by-products of this process are just plain nasty.

MIG (METAL INERT GAS) WELDING

The principle of Mig welding is that steel wire from a spool is fed through a torch. As it leaves the torch this wire is made live. Contact with an earthed workpiece creates an arc, and new metal (steel wire) is deposited to form the weld.

Atmospheric oxygen is purged from the weld area by a shielding gas (CO_2 or Argon CO_2 mix) issued from the same torch. By removing the oxygen from the weld area the new weld is not impaired by the formation of oxides that would otherwise create a brittle and weak joint.

In its simplest form, MIG welding requires very little skill or practice; a 'stud-weld,' as used to attach panels, can be produced in seconds. With a little guidance most people can create reasonable welds with this system. In skilled hands, MIG can be used for pretty much any welding job asked of it. In practice, MIG is the only method of welding that can be used in isolation, and is far and away the quickest method of joining steel other than the spot welder, which has other limitations.

It has to be pointed out that, because MIG relies on new metal being deposited at the site of weld, there will always be a build up of material. This build up will get in the way of some types of joint, particularly hammer-welding, and demands the removal of this excess in most cases. MIG wire is by nature a harder grade of steel than most of the panels which we will be repairing due to the demands of the wire transport system used to push the wire up to the torch.

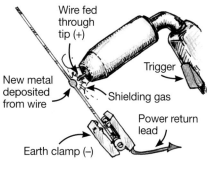

18-7. MIG welding detail.

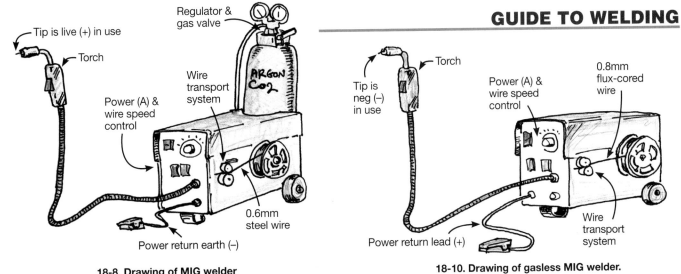

Tip is live (+) in use

Torch

Regulator & gas valve

Wire transport system

Power (A) & wire speed control

ARGON CO2

0.6mm steel wire

Power return earth (–)

18-8. Drawing of MIG welder

Torch

Tip is neg (–) in use

Power (A) & wire speed control

0.8mm flux-cored wire

Wire transport system

Power return lead (+)

18-10. Drawing of gasless MIG welder.

GASLESS MIG WELDING

Gasless MIG relies on a flux-cored wire to produce a shielding gas on contact with the arc. The advantages of gasless MIG are firstly that you obviously do not have to pay for gas. Less obvious, but more practical, is that the shielding gas is less likely to blow away in outdoor situations; making the gasless system a good choice for site work. The lack of a heavy gas bottle also helps greatly with portability. However, the downside is that the wire is far more costly than standard MIG wire, and this method creates a lot of nasty toxic smoke, plus the flux will leave a glazed residue on the weld, making over-welding more difficult.

Gasless welders differ when compared to the standard system in that the polarity is reversed. Dual polarity gas/no gas machines are available and offer greater flexibility at no extra cost. The 150amp SIP machine (shown) is a good all-round unit.

MIG welding aluminium is a practical option, as small reels of aluminium wire and disposable bottles of suitable gas are available from many high street outlets. Aluminium requires 25 per cent more power than steel to weld, and is more demanding in terms of skill because the

18-11. Gasless MIG is well suited to outdoor situations.

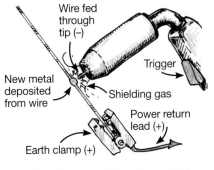

Wire fed through tip (–)

Trigger

New metal deposited from wire

Shielding gas

Power return lead (+)

Earth clamp (+)

18-9. Gasless MIG welding detail.

weld is reluctant to initiate, and when it does you have to work pretty fast to stop it blowing holes in the metal. Another quirk of this material is a tendency to distort some time after the process has been completed. Controlled cooling should be considered.

Cost & equipment

Domestic MIG welders are rated at between 100 and 180A and cost in the region of £150-£300. When selecting a welder you would do well to look at the 'duty-cycle,' often printed on the side of the machine. This will tell you what percentage of the time the machine is actually running at a given amperage. Stable power is far more important than big power in a domestic MIG, so at the lower outputs you would want to see your welder running

at 100 per cent. A good 130A machine is ample for our needs.

Shielding gas, usually Argon/Co2, can be supplied by BOC for a yearly rental cost for the bottle and paid for as used. I would suggest the Y-size cylinder at 93cm tall and 40kg or the X at the same height, but slimmer. This will cost about £60 for the rental and the same again for the gas. Alternatively, disposable bottles can be bought from many high street outlets at about £12-15 each or larger refillable bottles are available from Sealy for about £60, with subsequent refills costing about the same amount. As with most things, the economy is not always obvious and depends on exactly how much gas you are likely to use. If planning to do paid jobs for family and friends you may want to include the cost of a bottle each time. This may well provide you all the gas you will need. Learning to weld using disposable bottles will prove very costly.

MIG wire is supplied in 0.6 and 0.8mm copper-coated reels of 0.7kg and 5kg, expect to pay around £16 for 5kg of 0.6mm.

18-12. Reel of copper-coated 0.6mm wire.

18-13. Detail of wire transport system.

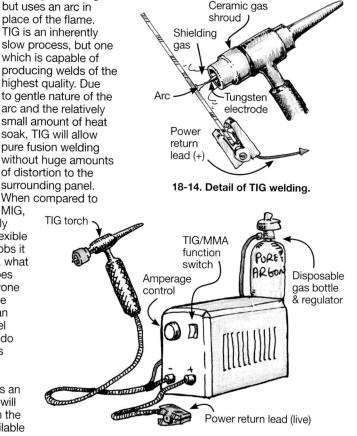

18-14. Detail of TIG welding.

18-15. Drawing of TIG welder.

Gasless wire is not available in 0.6mm, as this would not allow sufficient flux coring. Expect to pay about £45 for a 5kg reel of 0.8mm flux-cored wire.

For advice on buying a MIG, visit BOC or your local welding supply shop, or go to Welduk on the internet.

Another option is to buy a used machine – back in the '90s many people bought these things and left them under the stairs after just one use. Look out for a Cebora 130. If you find one, check it carefully and offer £50. These little wonders were unavailable for about a decade, but are now back in the shops priced at £250. They are good value at today's price and a bargain used.

Safety consideration for MIG welding

The MIG welder is a heavy, cumbersome machine with a gas bottle attached to it. It has a mains lead and produces a blinding arc and white hot sparks. Argon/Co2 is not toxic or flammable, in fact it acts as a fire extinguisher, but is by nature heavier than air and an oxygen depletor, and therefore an asphyxiant – never weld in a pit or closed space without proper extraction and ventilation.

Gasless MIG welders produce a lot of smoke containing gaseous ozone, which is known to cause delayed lung damage. Welding galvanized steel also produces some hazardous fumes.

TIG (TUNGSTEN INERT GAS) WELDING

TIG is a method of electrical welding in which an earthed tungsten electrode is held in close proximity to a work piece which is live and an arc exists between them. A shielding gas of pure argon is used to purge the weld area or atmospheric oxygen. The flow of gas also helps to cool the tungsten electrode and the molten weld. Any additional material for building or filling holes will have to be added as filler rod.

In practice, TIG welding is more akin to gas welding, but uses an arc in place of the flame. TIG is an inherently slow process, but one which is capable of producing welds of the highest quality. Due to gentle nature of the arc and the relatively small amount of heat soak, TIG will allow pure fusion welding without huge amounts of distortion to the surrounding panel. When compared to MIG, TIG is considerably slower and less flexible in terms of what jobs it can do. That said, what the TIG does it does very well, and anyone wishing to become a master craftsman in the field of panel fabrication would do well to get to grips with it.

TIG welding aluminium requires an AC welder, which will cost far more than the DC units now available for domestic use.

Costs & equipment

In recent years, a new generation of inverter TIG units have come onto the market, many based on MMA welders with a torch supplied separately. The latest machines from Parweld are complete TIG outfits with very high specification that feature the latest 'lift-TIG' starting system, which allows for easier initiation of the arc without any risk of heat build-up that can occur with lesser spec machines.

Look for a machine rated at 150A, and expect to pay in the region of £300 to get started. Pure Argon is available from BOC for approx £60 per year for rental of the bottle and a similar amount each time you collect a refill. Disposable bottles are available from many high street outlets, but these don't go very far using this process. In particular, you will find learning to weld with disposable bottles horribly expensive. At present, there is a fair bit of competition in this field, so shop around.

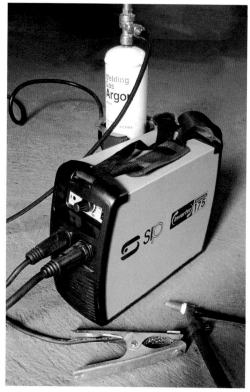

18-16. Typical inverter setup with mini gas bottle and TIG torch.

18-17. TIG welding.

Visit your local BOC shop or Welduk on the web.

Safety considerations for TIG welding

The TIG welder is a compact mains powered device with a torch, an earth lead and a gas bottle attached to it. In use, the system is live, but risk of injury caused by electric shock is minimal, although any person with a pacemaker or heart condition should take advice before using such gear.

The Argon shielding gas used in TIG is not flammable. In fact, it is a fire extinguisher, due to it being an oxygen depletor, which makes it an asphyxiant in concentration. Argon is heavier than air, so must not be used in a pit or confined space without proper ventilation and extraction. All welding fumes should be regarded as toxic.

The arc generated by the TIG process is obviously hazardous to the eyes without proper protection. Less obvious is the radiation damage it can cause to skin.

MMA (MANUAL METAL ARC)/ARC STICK WELDING

This is old-fashioned arc welding, but today's new inverter based machines are far easier to use and smoother in operation. In my opinion, MMA is not suitable for bodywork. In the hands of an experienced practitioner MMA is the most flexible and widely used system of joining steel available, but attempting to join thin sheet with an electrode measuring 20in, is like trying to paint the Mona Lisa with an ostrich feather!

RESISTANCE SPOT WELDING

The spot welder is covered in more detail in the Introduction (page 10), and only shown here as a brief comparison with the other methods available to you.

The resistance spot welder is an electrical device used to fuse nuggets of weld between two pieces of sheet steel. In use the process is very quick, demands no skill, and after the weld is complete it should require no further finishing. Add to this the fact that your car was put together on the production line using this very same process. Spot welding should be the obvious choice for restoration – but isn't!

Within the body shop trade a resistance spot welder has always been considered essential, despite the apparent ubiquity of the MIG. However, due to the fact that access to both sides of the work piece is required (unless you have a very expensive single-sided welder), the spot welder has to be used in conjunction with another method.

Where the spot welder can be used, it will save you hours when compared to the MIG and will pay for itself in days, if you value your time.

Cost & equipment

The cheapest way to acquire a decent spot welder is to approach a body shop that has upgraded, which most of them have. Expect to pay something like £100-150, and ask about the accessories.

New machines start at about £200 for a basic machine from Frost, or £600 from Sealy for a pro machine. There is also a 'fuzzy login' model (for a whopping £900) with HF function for aluminium or burning through paint.

Safety consideration for spot welding

The spot welder is a heavy and cumbersome machine, which feels a lot heavier after a few minutes of use. It is mains powered with a trailing lead and parts of it get very hot. It is possible to get an electric shock from these machines if you operate it whilst laying in a puddle and wearing a gold wedding band – I've seen it!

LEARNING TO WELD

Learning to weld is not something to be taken lightly and has great potential for damage to persons and property. For more information on what method or methods to opt for you might consider *Welding: a practical guide to joining metal* published by Crowood Press, which was written for this express reason.

Having decided which type of welder suits you, it would be a very good idea to get some professional instruction. Some technical colleges offer courses, or at worse you could approach a local tradesman.

ALTERNATIVE GAS SUPPLIES

For many years the supply of welding gas has been dominated by BOC Ltd, with its national network of outlets and delivery, and a comprehensive range of products. The company also stocks all the welding gear you might ever need, along with a wealth of expertise and sound advice.

In recent years some alternative suppliers of gas have surfaced, offering a limited but useful range of products. To benefit from the savings offered by some of these companies, you may be asked to buy a gas bottle outright and then pay for it to be refilled as required. This is all well and good, and indeed may allow large savings for some customers. Be warned though, that the transportation of pressurized gases is subject to some legal restrictions for safety sake. You cannot send gas bottles in the post or by standard courier, even if the gas in question is not toxic or explosive.

Appendix

Glossary of terms

A-post The upright member which continues from the side of the windscreen and usually supports the front door. Working from the front of the car the posts are listed as A, B, C, and D (if one is present). On an estate car (stationwagon) or hatchback, the rear pillar is called the D-post even if no C-post exists.

Angle-grinder or Grinderette Available in 4 or 4¹/₂in (100 or 115 mm). The angle grinder is one of the mainstays of the restoration game. Cutting, grinding and fibre disks are available, along with polishing and cleaning 'fleeces.' Newer 1mm (and thinner) cutting disks cut cleanly, accurately and easily.

Argon/CO2 A naturally occurring inert gas, argon is mixed with carbon dioxide in a variety of ratios, and is used as a shielding gas during MIG welding. In America, helium is often used for the same function.

Bodge A poorly carried-out, or deceitful repair (also botch).

Bodger A person of few ethics who would seek to carry out a sub-standard repair and pass it off as acceptable (also botcher).

Bogged-up Full of filler or other improper material.

Bonnet/hood The panel that sits over the engine at the front of the vehicle.

Box-section A closed section of metal, usually folded. May be produced by the addition of a three-sided member to a floor or other structure, as in the case of a chassis outrigger.

Box-folder or metal brake A device for forming bends or folds in sheet metal.

Boot/trunk The panel which closes the luggage compartment at the rear of the vehicle.

Bulkhead/firewall The panel which separates the engine compartment from the passengers.

Car Automobile.

Chassis Originally a separate structure which sat below the bodywork, the term chassis can now be applied to any structural or load-bearing piece of the vehicle. In particular, the term chassis rail is used to describe the two box-sections which run the length of the body under the floor. The term chassis leg is applied to the sections of rail forward of the passenger compartment which support the engine and suspension. When the term chassis leg is applied to the rear, things are even more confusing as this area is a straight continuation of the chassis rail!

Clag-up Clog-up.

Cold Front A proprietary ceramic paste used to control the spread of heat. It's very good.

Corrosion Rust or rusting.

Datum A fixed point from which to work to.

Dolly A form of hand-held anvil or beating block. The name goes back to the corn-dolly or idol.

Drop check A traditional low-tech method of checking the straightness of a vehicle's chassis. It involves dropping a plum bob from pairs of points along the chassis and marking their location on a level floor (see page 116).

Fettle To remove waste metal and tidy up a rough piece. This term was originally used by blacksmiths.

Flange An edge, face or feature designed to attach one piece to another.

Flitch plate Inner wing, the side panel of an engine bay.

Former A pattern or template used to produce a panel or section. May be used as a guide, or more directly, to influence the shaping.

Gash metal Waste metal, swarf, rust or surplus.

Grinder See Angle-grinder.

Hammer form A pattern which is beaten on, or against. Can be metal, wood or other resilient material.

Hammerite A proprietary brand of rust inhibiting paint which requires no primer; very popular with the restoration fraternity. Available in smooth and hammered finish.

Hot-shrinking A method involving heat used to reduce the surface area of a panel. This can be employed during repair or fabrication. Traditionally, the ability to hot-shrink was regarded as a key skill.

L-section A length of metal which is formed by two flat faces, each at right angles to the other, and connected along one edge.

Member A box-section or rail.

MIG (Metal Inert Gas) A form of welding which relies on a steel (usually) wire fed onto the workpiece. The workpiece is earthed (grounded) while the wire has a high voltage applied to it as it leaves the tip of the welder. The resulting arc deposits molten wire onto the workpiece. The job of the gas is to prevent the weld from oxidising.

MIG-spot A form of weld produced with the MIG welder. Strictly speaking, the MIG-spot is formed by the application of weld to two thicknesses of metal, the idea being that the weld will penetrate enough to fuse the two pieces. This term is often used to describe plug welding, which is similar, but involves a hole being drilled or punched through the top sheet of metal.

Monocoque A form of vehicle body which doesn't rely on a separate chassis. This term has become interchangeable with 'unitary,' though the original monocoque was more homogenous than many later designs, and the definition seems to have become obscured over time.

NS Nearside. The side of the vehicle that the driver doesn't sit on.

OS Offside. The side of the vehicle that the driver does sit on.

Outboard Away from the centre line of the vehicle.

Outrigger A box member or rail which comes off the main chassis toward the sill or other outboard structure.

PKs Self-tapping screws (after Parker Kingson). Used as temporary fixing.

Pattern Template or former, might be paper, wood, steel or other.

Petrol Gasoline.

Pop rivet A rivet which can be applied using a pop riveter. An ideal temporary fixing.

Porto-power A proprietary name for the commonly used hydraulic ram set common to the body shop trade. Available in 4 or 10 ton kits, this highly flexible and useful equipment has the capacity to inflict major damage to a vehicles structure. Use with care.

Pug Filler (also lard, wampum, plastic, crud, jollup, etc).

Pure argon A naturally occurring gas used to shield the arc in TIG welding, and for some MIG applications.

Rot Rust, corrosion, tin worm.

RQP Rear quarter panel, rear wing or fender.

Rust Ccorrosion specific to steel.

Sill Rocker panel, the member that runs below the doors.

Split & weld A modern philosophy of creating panels and repair sections from sheet metal whereby excess material is surgically removed, and new metal inserted. Traditionally, shrinking and hollowing techniques would have been used. The advantages of this newer method are speed of progress and a more even thickness to the finished piece.

Spot MIG A welding formed when a bead of molten metal is deposited in such a way as to join two sheets of metal. Usually the top piece has been drilled to allow for easier fusion, in which case this weld is more rightly called a plug weld.

Spot welder Resistance spot welder, an electrical device for forming spot welds by means of two electrodes and a voltage.

Spring hammer A flat blade of metal, usually with a cranked handle. This tool can be slapped against the workpiece, or used in conjuction with a heavy mallet or similar.

Sunshine wings A derogatory term used to describe insubstantial body panels.

Swager Beader. A device for forming swage lines and beads in panels; consists of upper and lower rolls (wheels) which impart shape when the piece is wound through them.

SWG Standard Wire Gauge – a traditional measure of metal thickness, or the tool used to find it. In Britain and Europe the metric system has now superseded SWG, though many of our cars will have been built using this standard.

Template A former or pattern. May be paper, steel, wood, or other.

TIG (Tungsten Inert Gas) A form of arc welding involving an earthed tungsten electrode and a workpiece that is made live by clamping a power return lead to it from the welding machine. Pure argon is used to purge the weld area of oxygen and cool the electrode.
TIG is a highly skilled and relatively slow process that can produce the highest quality of weld. Newer inverter machines have brought this method into the realms of the domestic.

Tin worm Rust.

Top-hat section A deep, U-section channel with a flange at the top. Often used to form chassis box-sections when closed by a floor.

Unitary construction A type of vehicle body which doesn't rely on a separate chassis.

Vice (Vise) A large clamp, usually bench-mounted.

Windscreen Windshield.

Index